The Inner Way

REFLECTIONS ON READING THE *INNER WAY* ANTHOLOGY

The Inner Way is a beautiful collection of unusual stories, inspiring poetry and fresh translations of ancient texts. For all who believe that "the kingdom of God is within," this small book will provide clarity and encouragement.

~ The Rev. Dr Barbara Merritt
Author, *Amethyst Beach*
Unitarian Universalist Minister (retd)

By turns evocative, startling, deeply moving and delightful, these poems, stories and quotations are an immensely valuable contribution to our global conversation about spirituality, meditative practice, cross-cultural religious studies and depth psychology. The sequence of the selections is a marvelous way of organizing such a poetic book.

~ Paul Moore, PhD
Psychologist, Lecturer, Writer

This informative and inspiring anthology is similar in tone and scope to Bede Griffiths, *Universal Wisdom: A Journey Through the Sacred Wisdom of the World*.... Anthea Guinness is emerging as a loving and trustworthy guide in helping persons of different faiths become one in their quest to know and experience the Truth.

~ William C. Bailey, PhD
Amazon review

I open this book and so often am moved to tears: the poetry, quotes and stories touch that deep place of yearning within.

~ Chloe Faith Wordsworth
Author, *Quantum change* and *Spiral Up!*
Founder, Resonance Repatterning

This book clearly spells out the fundamentals of spirituality. I believe it will uplift and move many hearts closer toward the inner essence and source that we all share.

~ Dr Berkeley Digby
Homeopathic physician, lover of Taoism

There is pleasure in reading fresh translations of songpoems by saints I've long appreciated – an enjoyment now complemented by quotations and stories from wisdom carriers new to me, as well as the editor's eloquent perspective.

~ Kenneth Frĕad
Woodworking craftsman, student of mysticism

I love that I can keep this book close by, open to any page, and find something juicy to ponder. The Perspective pages, author index and glossary are essential to the neophyte (like me) and help make *The Inner Way* a significant source for personal and group study.

~ Shanan Harrell
Author, *Stumbling towards enlightenment*

Opening *The Inner Way* connects the reader to the heart of spirituality and the mystery of longing, seeking and merging beyond the boundaries of language, religion and time. Each poem is enhanced by stories and sayings from mystics of all ages, offering a unique invitation to join the celebration of love.

~ Farida Sharan, ND
Author, *The old man and his soul*
Founder, School of Natural Medicine

Other translations by Anthea Guinness

Wake up! if you can: Sayings of Kabir with reflections and mystic stories

Soami Ji of Agra answering questions: Mystic teachings on the path of inner sound, 2 *volumes*

POCKETBOOK *Dawn has come: Songpoems of Paltu*

the inner way

A MYSTIC ANTHOLOGY
of songpoems, stories, reflections

arranged with translations and notes
by Anthea Guinness

SR SALT RIVER

GLOBAL LIBRARY
is an imprint of Salt River Publishing
Phoenix, Arizona
www.SaltRiverPublishing.com

First edition

19 18 17 14 13 12 III II I

ISBN 978-0-9893349-0-7

Cover photo by Rune Clausen *(see Colophon)*, used with permission: The Long Man, Wilmington, on the South Downs, England

Publisher discount available
www.SaltRiverPublishing.com/estore/

CONTENTS

Mystic Exploration 1

Reality 29
The Path 56
The Master 82
The Mystery 107
Yearning 131
Love 155
Union 180

Glossary 185
Authors 189
Stories 194

Endnotes 195
Browsing 209
Acknowledgements 213

The photo on the cover is of The Long Man on the South Downs of southeast England, about five miles from the coast. Seen from the foot of the hill, this giant figure is fully in proportion, etched into the turf on a steep hillside below an ancient barrow that dates, some say, to the neolithic period.

The Long Man in this book of mystic writings represents the seeker within each one of us – the wanderer, wise one, warrior; the mystic, the lover, the fool.

Known locally in earlier centuries as The Green Man, he also represents that eternal presence on earth – the living master, the bringer of spiritual light, the guide on the ascent through the inner worlds of consciousness to the land of our spiritual origins.

Giant of a man, visible for miles around, he both awes and inspires. He touches our innermost being and fills us with longing. Impelled, we search for him within, struggling up the mountain of consciousness – because somewhere inside, above the eyes, is where he waits for us.

High on the hill, Wise One, Warrior, Friend and Fool, he is the Beloved.

Long Man, Green Man: seeker, Sought. The meeting of these two is what the inner way is all about.

MYSTIC EXPLORATION

As human beings we have a unique capacity: to expand our consciousness to its infinite potential. The mystics do not say this is easy. But they assure us it is possible – even for all of us ordinary people immersed in our everyday lives, caught up in the busyness of the modern world and endowed with no exceptional spiritual gifts.

Mystic writings are a reminder that men and women everywhere, each seeking the sacred within themselves, have embarked on heroic inner journeys towards higher consciousness. Their example and their words encourage us: if other people have attempted realization, so can we!

The Inner Way highlights seven aspects of the path of devotion. Using songpoems from the teachings of north Indian mystics interwoven with stories and reflections from many other traditions, the anthology tells the timeless story of mystic exploration. Recorded in different parts of the world by writers ancient, medieval and contemporary, the stories and reflections include insights from the Hindu, Taoist, Buddhist, early Egyptian, Hebrew, classical Greek, Native American, Jewish, Christian, Islamic and Sikh traditions.

The reason for juxtaposing these wide-ranging selections is not to promote the idea that all mystic teachings are identical, although in fact there are common threads that emerge in spiritual traditions everywhere. Rather, it is to celebrate the wealth of mystic insights that have come down to us over the last several thousand years from different peoples of the world.

Devotional masters have existed throughout all traditions, and so has the following of an inner path towards realization of the spiritual mysteries. But the writings in the Naam bhakti mystic tradition – including the songpoems presented in the *Inner Way* anthology – are exceptionally consistent, clear and focused with regard to the fundamental principles and practice of the way of inner devotion. These writings may even lead us towards a deeper understanding of our own as well as other mystic traditions, ancient and medieval, that are shrouded now by distance and time.

Mystic beginnings

As a spiritual teaching, Naam bhakti maps a way towards realization of Naam, the Name: the mysterious essence of all things.

The bhakti mystics speak of love and devotion, and of the immense grace of experiencing a longing for more than we find in the material world. They say that something within us pulls us, calls us, and we start looking. For what? We're not sure, but on some level we know it is love, *prém, ishq* – real love, everlasting love. According to the medieval Punjabi mystic Farid, intense longing is the emperor of all paths. At any stage, longing is the force that pulls and impels our consciousness on the inward journey – towards divine love, light and understanding.

The mystics remind us of our purpose and potential as human beings. While we are alive, they say we have an opportunity to set out on the path towards fulfilment of that longing for love, the yearning for wholeness. Their writings invite us to turn within – to settle into a receptive place where the waves of the mind quieten and we begin to experience an inkling of the longing for the divine Beloved that consumes these lovers whose words have survived the centuries.

Speaking from their own experience, the mystics encourage us that there is a way to seek and to knock at the door of the Beloved: meditation. They tell us we need to find a true spiritual guide, a living master, who can show us how to meditate on the divine essence. And then we need to go on knocking at that inner door for the rest of our life.

The on-going meditation practice establishes an inner relationship with one's spiritual teacher. It is a relationship of love that is kindled, strengthened and expressed through this inward form of devotion or *bhakti* – meditation. Once the teacher-disciple relationship is established, the rest, they say, follows automatically: full awakening, realization of absolute oneness.

As a pedestrian on the spiritual path, the ordinary meditator continues to experience pain and pleasure, attachment and loss, birth, death and disappointment – even devastation. But initiation by a true teacher implants something that nothing can destroy: the seed of divine love. Mira, a woman mystic from the 1500s, warns that the seed of love grows into a huge tree that cannot be hidden, suppressed or cut down.

Alone and unaided, we could not begin to bring about this total transformation of our consciousness. For the masters, however, it is simple: "Uproot from here and transplant there," as the gardener Inayat Shah tells his disciple Bullah. That inward movement may not feel quick or easy, from the disciple's point of view. Any big undertaking challenges us to make a day-in, day-out commitment; the spiritual path is no different, say the mystics.

Whether meditation is experienced as the lifeline it is or as the struggle we may turn it into, the mystics say it is the birthing of an extraordinary love relationship – a relationship that accompanies us beyond our last breath. As the outspoken medieval mystic Kabir says, This is the home of love we're talking about, not a visit to your auntie's – it demands your ego, the sum total of everything you hold dear.

Time well spent, says a twentieth-century mystic. Why? In a verse from the 1700s, Paltu explains: If we win the game of love, we get the Beloved; if we lose – he gets us!

About the book

The Inner Way is divided into seven thematic sections that, taken together, offer a sense of the great undertaking, the adventure and the revelation of the mystic journey.

- Reality
- The Path
- The Master
- The Mystery
- Yearning
- Love
- Union

Each section begins with a definition or gist of the theme, followed by a detailed table of contents. The selections include songpoems as well as sayings and stories, arranged loosely by these seven themes rather than by author, century or religious tradition.

The idea for the supporting quotes and stories was to provide a lively commentary, expanding on topics mentioned in the songpoems; what we didn't foresee was the "conversation" that would result. The mystic commentary we hoped for took off in new directions, reverberating all the way: on one page you may find a medieval mystic and a modern story both addressing the same issue, and in any one section you'll find more than a dozen mystics from different centuries with completely different backgrounds discussing one theme, coming at it from various points of view.

The Hindi and Punjabi compositions in this book come from mystics who lived in the pre-modern period in India, from the 1200s to the 1800s, when reading and writing were rare. Songpoems and singing were the common medium for recording and communicating mystic teachings – songs and rhyming poetry being much easier than prose to memorize, sing and recite. Even today, Indians everywhere sing and recite by heart the writings of those earlier mystics.

The verses of the Indian mystics are composed somewhat like lyrics for a song: the rhythm, the number of beats or syllables in each line, the pairing of lines into couplets, and the rhyming words at the end of the lines are all designed to make it possible to sing the poems to standard, well-known tunes. These *shabds* (words), as the mystics call them, and the brief, memorable 4-line *saakhis* or *dohas* (teaching sayings) were not passed on in written form but by singing and reciting them, one person to the next. In one way or another, then, the mystics' compositions are not exactly songs or poems, but a combination of the two – referred to in this book as songpoems.

As for the stories in *The Inner Way*, while most of them are closely associated with particular mystics, the English renderings are just one more retelling of these meaningful tales. When you tell a story the words shift and change as you speak, especially when the story is a translation from another language, another culture, another era. The original sources on which the stories are based, when available, are given in the endnotes.

Can you read and enjoy *The Inner Way* without any knowledge of the spiritual traditions the selections come from? Yes. And for readers who would like to go a little deeper into the mystic context of the songpoems, it may be helpful to look at the "Perspective" pages and the Glossary.

For more information on the Naam bhakti tradition, *Soami Ji of Agra Answering Questions: Mystic Teachings on the Path of Inner Sound* may be useful, as also some of the titles listed in the Browsing section. For other mystic traditions, the source books are listed in the endnotes so that readers can follow up easily on anything that catches their attention.

Nearly all the authors cited in the anthology are mystics, which raises the issue of how to refer to them: by their birth name, by an assumed name, by an honorary title, or by including a saintly prefix and suffix. In many languages and cultures, mystics past and present are referred to respectfully with titles and devout expressions, but in the West we are more comfortable referring to Moses, Jesus, Krishna and other revered teachers of the past, including Nanak, Rumi and Kabir, without any title at all, keeping simple titles for contemporary teachers.

Most of the authors in this book are identified in the secular English style, by name; no disrespect is meant in doing so. A few of the authors are better known by an assumed name or a title: in those cases the names reflect common usage.

The wife of the Beloved

One characteristic of mystic verse in India is the way the saints sometimes write in the female voice – obvious in the Hindi/Punjabi because the verb forms are unambiguously feminine. In shabds on yearning and union in particular, the bhakti mystics frequently address the Beloved as though they were a woman: usually as the wife or bride of the Beloved; occasionally as his lover, child, servant girl or slave.

Are we to take these poems literally, at times even as expressions of physical passion? Certainly many Western scholars and readers unfamiliar with mysticism have done so over the centuries – whether discussing the Rubaiyat of Omar

Khayyam, the poetry of Hafiz or the relationship of Rumi and his spiritual teacher Shams. But do we not miss the point entirely when we interpret mystic writers in that way?

The love poetry of the mystics bears extraordinary witness to the various stages of spiritual evolution in the teacher-disciple relationship and to their oneness with the divine. The love affair and the union they speak of are not sexual and cannot be put into words, but by using human images of passionate undying love and longing the mystics evoke for us an echo of the intensity of what they experience. The bhakti mystics invite and indeed entice us to become the wife of the one Beloved – that elusive Lover and godlike Bridegroom the mystics describe as the soul's magnificent Husband, here and now, for eternity.

My hope is that *The Inner Way* provides basic information about the Naam bhakti mystic tradition – and that readers, regardless of their own particular backgrounds, will be inspired and encouraged in their inner practice by these reflections from mystics around the world.

Reality

Life as a dream –
passing pain and pleasure.
The purpose of life.
Perspectives on permanence:
the inner reality.

1. **Ravidas**
This world p.12
ihu jag dukh ki khétari
- Shunryu Suzuki: Life is like getting into a boat
- Nirvana ~ A story
- Luther Standing Bear: Wait and listen
- The Mother: A total conversion
- Ibn Ata'illah: Zikr is a fire

2. **Tegh Bahadur**
Like a dream or a show p.14
jiu supana ar/u pékhana
- Letting go ~ A story
- Bassui Zenji: What is obstructing realization?
- Plato: Reflections in a cave
- Pema Chödrön: Beyond dreams

3. **Kabir**
This is the home of love we're talking about p.17
yaha to ghar hai prém ka
- Gerhard Tersteegen: He who is
- Idries Shah: Nasruddin ~ A story
- One penny ~ A story
- Rabindranath Tagore: Only thee

4. **Guru Arjan**
The goods you came here to collect p.20
jis vakhar ka'u lain too aa'ia
- Walter Raleigh: Trust
- The seeker's dream ~ A story
- Aurobindo: The greater reality
- Jesus: The light of the body is the eye

5. **Tulsi of Hathras**
This heart of yours p.23
dil ka hujra saaf kar
- Gerhard Tersteegen: A little secret room
- Black Elk: The heart is a sanctuary
- Shibli and Junayd: The pearl
- *The Cloud of Unknowing:* Always be at this work
- Shams: Neediness

6. **Kabir**
My house? I've burnt it down p.27
ham ghar jaara aapana
- The Desert Fathers: What more should I do?
- Chuang-tse: Flying without wings
- Abraham Isaac Kook: The flame of the holy fire

Perspective p.29

Ravidas

1414–1540

Everybody knows
This world is a field of suffering.
The wise pick a harvest of God's Name;
Fools reap everything but – with tears.[1]

Shunryu Suzuki

1904–1971

Life is like getting into a boat that's just about to sail out to sea and sink.[2]

Nirvana ~ A story

400s BCE

A disciple came to the Buddha and asked, "How many lifetimes will it take me to reach nirvana?" and the Buddha told him: As many as there are leaves on this tree. "Oh no, so many?" And he turned away, dejected.

The Buddha smiled.

Another disciple came to the Buddha and asked the same question: "How many lifetimes will it take me to reach nirvana?" and the Buddha told him: As many as there are leaves on this tree. "Really? So few!" And he leapt up joyfully, dancing.

The Buddha smiled.

And took the disciple beyond time and space.[3]

Luther Standing Bear — *1868–1939*

Children are taught to go directly to the source of the Great Mystery. In order that knowledge does not get separated from experience or wisdom from divinity, wait and listen. Do not ask why. A child that cannot sit still is a half-developed child.[4]

The Mother — *1878–1973*

In the old Chaldean tradition, very often the young novices were given an image when they were invested with the white robe; they were told: "Do not try to remove the stains one by one, the whole robe must be purified."

Do not try to correct your faults one by one, to overcome your weaknesses one by one – it does not take you very far. The entire consciousness must be changed, a reversal of consciousness must be achieved: a springing up out of the state in which one is towards a higher state from which one dominates all the weaknesses one wants to heal, and from which one has a full vision of the work to be accomplished.

I believe Sri Aurobindo said this: Nothing is done until everything is done. One step ahead is not enough; a total conversion is necessary.[5]

Ibn Ata'illah — *1200s–1309*

Zikr, repeating spiritually evocative names, is a fire. If it finds wood, it burns it; if it finds darkness, it changes it into light; if it finds light, it adds more and more light to the light.[6]

Tegh Bahadur 1621–1675

Like a dream or a show:
That's the world – get it!
Nothing in it is real, Nanak,
Except God.[7]

Letting go ~ A story *Traditional*

A man was out walking one morning when he tripped at the top of a cliff. He fell over the edge but managed to catch hold of a small tree growing out of a crevice in the rock.

Terrified, he yelled out: "Help!" Nobody heard him. So he shouted, "God, please help me!"

A sonorous voice immediately replied: "All right – let go and I'll catch you."

There was a moment's silence and then the man peered up at the sky and said, "Is there someone else up there?"[8]

Bassui Zenji *1327–1387*

What is obstructing realization? Nothing but your own half-hearted desire for truth. Think of this and exert yourself to the utmost.[9]

Plato *424–347* BCE

Picture some people dwelling in a subterranean cavern with a long entrance open to the light on its entire width. Imagine their legs and necks have been fettered since childhood, so they remain in the same spot, able to look only forward, prevented by the fetters from turning their heads.

Picture also the light from a fire, burning higher up and at a distance behind them; and between the fire and the prisoners and above them a road along which a low wall has been built, much like the partition between puppeteers and the audience, above which you see the puppets.

People walk along the road, carrying implements of all kinds that rise above the wall, and human images and shapes of animals as well, made in stone and wood and every material, some of these bearers speaking and others silent.

Do you think the prisoners would have seen anything of themselves or of one another except the shadows cast from the fire onto the wall of the cave that faces them? And would not the same be true of the objects carried past them?

And if their prison had an echo from the wall facing them, when one of the passers-by uttered a sound, do you think they would suppose the speaker was anything other than the passing shadow?

In every way such prisoners would suppose reality to be these shadows of artificial objects![10]

Pema Chödrön *1936–*

There is a teaching on the three kinds of awakening: awakening from the dream of ordinary sleep, awakening at death from the dream of life, and awakening into full enlightenment from the dream of delusion. These teachings say that when we die, we experience it as waking up from a very long dream.

If all this is really a dream, I might as well spend it trying to look at what scares me instead of running away.

The first time I met my teacher, Chögyam Trungpa Rinpoche, a small boy asked him if he was ever afraid. Rinpoche answered that his teacher had encouraged him to go to places like graveyards that scared him and to experiment with approaching things he didn't like.

Then he told about travelling with his attendants to a monastery he'd never seen before. As they neared the gates, he saw a large guard dog with huge teeth and red eyes. It was growling ferociously and struggling to get free from the chain that held it. The dog seemed desperate to attack them. As Rinpoche got closer, he could see its bluish tongue and spittle spraying from its mouth.

They walked past the dog, keeping their distance, and entered the gate. Suddenly the chain broke and the dog rushed at them. The attendants screamed and froze in terror. Rinpoche turned and ran as fast as he could – straight at the dog. The dog was so surprised that he put his tail between his legs and ran away.

The spiritual journey involves going beyond hope and fear, stepping into unknown territory, continually moving forward. The most important aspect of being on the spiritual path may be to just keep moving.[11]

Kabir

1398–1518

This is the home of love we're talking about,
Not a visit to your auntie's:
You've got to cut off your head, my friend,
And stick it on the ground –
Then, says Kabir, you can step inside.

I swear love came – now where's it gone?
Everybody saw it. Says Kabir,
Crying one minute, laughing the next –
You think that's love?

Without love – no patience.
Without longing – self-discipline.
Without a true teacher – it will not go, Kabir,
This stain on the mind of desire.

What we see doesn't exist;
What is can't be put into words.
Without seeing there's no faith, Kabir –
And those who've seen are silent.[12]

Gerhard Tersteegen *1697–1769*

We see, we admire, we bury ourselves in things that are not, and he who is, we leave out of consideration.

God is more inward than our most intimate thought. There he calls us, there he waits for us. He wants to impart himself to us and make us blessed.[13]

Nasruddin ~ A story *Traditional*

Mullah Nasruddin stood up in the marketplace and started to address the throng:

"O people! Do you want knowledge without difficulty, attainment without effort, progress without sacrifice?"

Very soon a large crowd gathered, everyone shouting: "Yes, yes!"

"Excellent!" said the Mullah. "I only wanted to know. You may rely on me to tell you all about it if I ever discover any such thing."[14]

One penny ~ A story *1960s*

In the 1960s, a spiritual teacher came for two days of satsang in Mandi, Himachal Pradesh, a mountainous region in north India. Hundreds of villagers from all the surrounding areas walked, bused and caught rides on tractor-trailers to reach Mandi and attend this special event.

To the surprise of the organizers, the master indicated that after satsang on the second day, he would sit and accept monetary offerings (séva) for the use of the sangat, or congregation.

An announcement was made to this effect and the next day a long line formed with several thousand people who wished to contribute. Almost at the front of the line was an old lady in her eighties. She slowly came forward, put down the package she was carrying and squatted down near the master's feet to open it.

The organizers began to hurry her up, but the master gestured, saying: "Let her do what she wants."

Unconcerned, the old lady undid the knot holding together the cotton cloth of her small bundle. As she opened up the cloth, another knotted bundle was revealed inside, and when that was opened, another inside that.

Eventually, after untying and opening up a dozen of these kerchiefs, she took a very small coin from the innermost handkerchief and put it into the collection box.

The old lady's eyes filled with tears. Clasping her hands in gratitude, she said, "Master, I have been waiting twenty years to give this in séva. I couldn't make the journey to where you live, so all this time I have been waiting to give it to you in person."

Looking intently into her eyes, the master nodded gently and thanked her. Unhurried, he stood up, glanced affectionately at the expectant people in the line, bowed and walked away.[15]

Rabindranath Tagore *1861–1941*

That I want thee, only thee – let my heart repeat without end. All desires that distract me, day and night, are false and empty to the core.

As the night keeps hidden in its gloom the petition for light, even thus in the depth of my unconsciousness rings the cry – I want thee, only thee.

As the storm still seeks its end in peace when it strikes against peace with all its might, even thus my rebellion strikes against thy love and still its cry is – I want thee, only thee.[16]

Guru Arjan

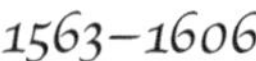

1563–1606

The goods you came here to collect,
This Name of God,
You'll find it in the house of the saints.

Drop your ego, pay the price, mind,
And weigh out God's Name in your heart.
Load up to the brim,
Set out in the caravan of the saints –
Leave everything else behind: it's poison, a trap.

Everybody will say how blessed you are,
Your face radiant in the court of the Lord –
But how rare the traders who deal in these goods:
Nanak happily gives his life for people like that![17]

Walter Raleigh

1554–1618

Written in prison, shortly before his execution

Even such is Time, which takes in trust
   Our youth, our joys, and all we have,
And pays us but with age and dust:
   Who in the dark and silent grave,

When we have wandered all our ways,
Shuts up the story of our days:
And from which earth and grave and dust
The Lord shall raise me up, I trust.[18]

The seeker's dream ~ A story *Contemporary*

Once, a man had a dream that he met a holy man at dusk at the edge of a forest who gave him a precious stone.

He hurried to the wooded area on the outskirts of his village that evening and sure enough, there sat a sadhu.

"Please give me the stone!" said the villager, forgetting to greet the ascetic in his eagerness.

"Which stone do you mean?"

"I dreamt that you gave me a precious stone," he explained.

"Ah, perhaps it's the stone I found on my way here," said the sadhu. He casually reached into his tattered cloth shoulder bag and held out on the palm of his hand a huge diamond that glowed in the fading light.

"Thank you, kind sir," stammered the man as he took the diamond and hurried back home.

At dawn the next day, the man returned to the sadhu, who was quietly meditating at the edge of the forest. "What can I do for you, my friend?" asked the sadhu, opening his eyes.

"I couldn't sleep all night! Please – take back this diamond and give me the other wealth you have!"

"But I don't have any wealth, brother."

"Oh yes, you do. Why else would it be so easy for you to give away a priceless diamond? Please – that's the treasure I want: show me how to find it."[19]

Aurobindo *1872–1950*

Spirituality is in its essence an awakening to the inner reality of our being, to a spirit, self, soul that is other than our mind, life and body – an inner aspiration to know, to feel, to be that, to enter into contact with the greater reality beyond and pervading the universe, which inhabits also our own being; to be in communion with it and union with it, and a turning, a conversion, a transformation of our whole being as a result of the aspiration, the contact, the union: a growth or waking into a new becoming or new being; a new self, a new nature.

> A secret sense awoke that could perceive
> A Presence and a Greatness everywhere.
> The universe was not now this senseless whirl
> Borne round inert on an immense machine
> ...But a living movement of the body of God.[20]

Jesus *100s*

The lamp of the body is the eye. So if your eye is single, your whole body will be full of light. But if your eye is diseased, your whole body will be full of darkness.

And if the light within you is darkness, how dark that is![21]

Tulsi of Hathras

1700s–1843

This heart of yours,
Meditation sanctuary hidden within –
Clean it out for the Beloved to come!
Bring back your attention
From all this otherness
If you want him to sit here.

Look with your mind's eye
At the fantastic shows going on:
Everything geared to captivating your heart –
Endlessly enticing!

One heart – a million desires,
And even more cravings on top of that.
What quiet place is there for him
If you want him to settle here?

How sad – we bring about our own suffering
By going to man-made temples and mosques
When we're living right inside
The Creator's mosque!

Go deep, listen attentively
Inside the prayer niche
Of this natural Ka'ba: All the way

From the primal beginning-place
The call is coming –
Inviting you, calling you home.

Why are you wandering around
Lost and confused,
All in search of the Friend?
The path to that ravisher of hearts
Is inside Shaah Rug, the royal vein.

Meet the complete master, Taqi –
With patience and sincerity.
He will give you the understanding
To find the royal vein inside.

Your inner ear will open
After you practise a few days –
You'll go from "There is no God"
To the Great One himself!

This is Tulsi's call:
You are a practitioner –
Do the practice… with attention.
Kun, "Be!", God's primal Word,
Stands for the Supreme Lord of all.
So it is written in the Qur'an.[22]

Gerhard Tersteegen *1697–1769*

It is as if there were a little secret room in your heart where your best friend lives and waits for you. And so your love must urge you now and then to purchase some time and if possible some outward loneliness so you can go to your friend in the little room and talk to him privately, and tell him how you are and that you want to love him truly.

And when you go back again to your business, let it be as if you took your friend by the hand and begged him to come with you and while you work keep you company and take care of you. And that he will do most willingly![23]

Black Elk *1863–1950*

The heart is a sanctuary at the center of which there is a little space wherein the Great Spirit dwells, and this is the eye. This is the eye of the Great Spirit by which he sees all things, and through which we see him. If the heart is not pure, the Great Spirit cannot be seen.[24]

Shibli and Junayd *800s*

Shibli sought out Junayd as a teacher and said to him, "Many people have informed me that you are a supreme expert on the pearls of awakening and divine wisdom. Either give me one of these pearls or sell one to me."

Junayd smiled. "If I sell you one, you won't be able to pay the price; if I give you one, coming by it so easily will drive you to undervalue it. Do like me: dive headfirst into the Sea. If you wait patiently, you will obtain your pearl."[25]

The Cloud of Unknowing *1300s*

You should always be at this work, both on duty and off, in intention if not in reality. This work demands great serenity, an integrated and pure disposition, in soul and in body.[26]

Shams *1184–1247*

If you remove your attention from your body and vacate it, you have still only reached another part of this creation. Because Truth is not created, how can the created find the Uncreated?

When such a magnanimous court exists and he is so free of need, you can take your need to him, for those without need enjoy the needy drawing near.

Thus, you suddenly leap out of the midst of these inferior surroundings through your neediness. Something beyond this creation will reach you – and that is love. The snare of love comes and wraps around you, for "They love Him" (Qur'an 5:54) is the effect of "He loves them" (Qur'an 5:54). You will see what is beyond this creation, through itself: "And He pervades the eyes" (Qur'an 6:103).

This is the entire talk; yet it will never reach an end, not even if you talk until resurrection day.[27]

Kabir

1398–1518

My house? I've burnt it down.
I've got a blazing torch in my hand
And I'm off to set fire
To the house of anybody
Who wants to come with me![28]

The Desert Fathers

300s

Abbot Lot came to Abbot Joseph and said: Father, according as I am able, I keep my little rule, and my little fast, my prayer, meditation and contemplative silence; and according as I am able, I strive to cleanse my heart of thoughts. Now what more should I do?

The elder rose up in reply and stretched out his hands to heaven, and his fingers became like ten lamps of fire. He said, Why not be totally changed into fire?[29]

Chuang-tse

400s BCE

Confucius said, "It is easy to stand still and leave no trace, but it is hard to walk without touching the ground. If you follow human methods, you can get away with deception. In the way of Tao, no deception is possible.

"You know that one can fly with wings. You have not yet learned to fly without wings. You are familiar with the wisdom of those who know, but you have not yet learned the wisdom of those who know not.

"Look at this window: it is nothing but a hole in the wall, but because of it the whole room is full of light. So when the faculties are empty, the heart is full of light. Being full of light it becomes an influence by which others are secretly transformed."[30]

Abraham Isaac Kook *1865–1935*

The flame of the holy fire of the love of God is always burning in the human heart. It is this that warms the human spirit and illumines life; the delights it yields are endless – there is no measure by which to assess it.

But how cruel is man towards himself that he allows himself to be sunk in the dark abyss of life, troubles himself with petty considerations, while he erases from his mind this that spells true life, the basis for all that gives meaning to life.

All this is contrary to the nature of life; indeed it is contrary to the nature of existence. The grace of God's love, a boon from On High, is destined to break out from its confinements, and the holiness of life will hew a path towards this delight, so as to enable it to appear in its full splendour and might.

"No eye has seen what God alone will do for those who wait for him" (Bible, *Isaiah* 64:3).[31]

PERSPECTIVE

Why do all mystics say, like Tegh Bahadur, that life is a dream and the world is not real? Why, like Kabir, do they say that what we see doesn't exist? For us the world is very real, what we see is solid reality, and we take it for granted we are wide awake.

Through a process of refining and attuning the attention, it seems the mystics have realized a more comprehensive or expanded state of consciousness than most of us can lay claim to. Ordinary human consciousness has a limited span of physical perception only and no perception of any subtle dimensions. What we think of as being awake looks to the mystics like deep unconscious sleep because they live in "reality" – a transcendent state characterized by omnipresence, omniscience, complete tranquillity and, for want of a better word, bliss.

Mystic teachers give years of their life to helping and encouraging people to wake up and discover what Tulsi calls the "meditation sanctuary hidden within." They offer to show us how to enter this threshold to higher consciousness so we can go at will beyond the limitations of the physical body, the mind and intellectual knowledge – "all this otherness" that is not who we are – in order to experience within ourselves what eternally is: reality.

To live in the subtle, more expanded consciousness of reality, the mystics say we need to reduce our attention on the outer world and turn our attention inside. For most people this is not acceptable; for the rest of us, it's not easy. The mystics warn that following the inner path is going to challenge and even require the surrender of the ego: You've got to cut off your head, my friend, says Kabir – to attain the essence of reality, which he calls love.

What is surrendering the ego and setting out in the caravan of the saints, as Guru Arjan advises us to? In down-to-earth terms, the meditation practice (travelling in the caravan or company of the mystic teacher) requires what the ego finds hard to give: time, effort and attention. Putting aside the ego's objections, one needs to keep going daily on that interior journey towards greater consciousness – practising patiently, persistently, in the face of failure to hold the focus inside. In the final analysis, it is the teacher's pleasure at the student's continued efforts and not the student's success that will kindle the blazing fire of divine love, enabling one to live fully in reality.

Love may start as a small flame but it transforms the meditation practice. From mere obedience, discipline and routine it becomes stillness, receptivity and focus. Continuing to give time regardless of feeling any progress strengthens the love, allowing for the unfolding of a process that lifts one above I-ness. It frees the practitioner from the limitations of body and mind, to discover the subtle dimensions beyond.

As the student goes within what the bhakti mystics call the heart or eye centre, the inner sanctuary, they say one begins to wake up to a more consistent awareness of inner peace, or the inner light and sound. That awakening of consciousness leads eventually to the joy of meeting what Sufis call "the ravisher of hearts" – the beautiful radiant form of the living master, the inner guide.

And that is when faith and awareness of reality begin.

The Path

The living master,
the Great Mystery,
and the gift of initiation.
Establishing the daily practice
and living the life of a disciple
while participating fully in the world.
The process: keeping going –
focusing on effort, not results.

1. **Soami Ji of Agra**
The master says it clearly p.34
guru kahé~ khol kar bhaa'i
- Abdisho Hazzaya: The subtle sound
- Juan de la Cruz: Human knowledge is not sufficient
- Jilani: Nothing but remembrance
- Donkey mind ~ A story

2. **Kabir**
The Creator is everywhere p.38
khaalik khoobai khoob hai
- Abu Sa'id Ibn Abi'l Khayr: Spiritual hunger
- Plato: A time of adjustment
- Lahiji: Give up your place
- *Mundaka Upanishad:* Two birds, mirror images

3. **Tulsi of Hathras**
Do not go searching outside p.42
sun ai taqi na jaa'iyo zinhaar dékhna
- Eckhart: You need not look for God
- Chuang-tse: Obstructions
- Aurobindo: Inward concentration
- Eugen Herrigel: Awa Kenzo and the earthquake

4. **Farid**

Axe on shoulder, waterpot on head p.47
kaNDh/u kuhaaRa sir ghaRa

- Shams: Knowledge or action
- Yellow ribbons ~ A story
- Pema Chödrön: The lion's roar
- Coventry Patmore: A gnat

5. **Guru Arjan**

Through simran of the Lord p.50
prabh kai simaran/i kaaraj pooré

- Laurent de la résurrection: Continual conversation
- Nancy Pope Mayorga: A conspiracy
- The modern disciple ~ A story
- The Buddha: Conquering the self

6. **Paltu**

There was this other Paltu p.53
doosar palaTu ik raha

- Dov Baer: I found a light in a closet
- *Hadith Qudsi:* The humble heart
- Shams: The oyster and the pearl ~ A story
- The Mother: Wake up – then conquer

Perspective p.56

Soami Ji of Agra

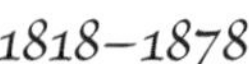

1818–1878

The master says it clearly: My friend,
Attach yourself to the unending sound.
Apart from Shabd there is no other way
To break out of this narrow-necked water bottle!

The master shows you the home
Within the home
And tells you about the melody, the five sounds.
Attach yourself to the sound current, the Dhun:
From this home, go to that home!

That home is immeasurable –
Limitless, no boundaries –
You'll see it when you've passed the tenth.
Climb up inside this body of ten doors
And open the gateway within:
In that inner space, experience for yourself
Sat Shabd, the true Word.

Without grace, you won't meet a master;
Without Shabd, you won't attain anything.
Pull your attention together so you climb
To the inner sky, and then listen
To the melody of Shabd. This is your task.

Restless mind never keeps still,
So how will it ever become clean?

Do the practice of Surat Shabd –
Merge consciousness in Sound.
Forget about all other efforts!
Give it your full conviction –
Don't wander off out of laziness.

I have sung of the essence of the essence,
Told about the path of the saints.
I have revealed the secret of Radha Soami,
    Lord of the soul:
Hear it, accept it.
I have explained the essential.[32]

Abdisho Hazzaya *700s*

We say we see light in the spiritual realms, but that light is not like our material light. We say also we have there a spiritual food, but that food is not like the one we have here. We say further that our mind will perceive there the sound of the glorification of the spiritual hosts and that it will there have speech and conversation – but that speech does not resemble what we hold with one another here.

The sound heard there by our mind is so subtle our senses are not able to receive it, and this physical tongue is not able to put into words what is made manifest there to the mind, whether it be through our seeing or our hearing.

Blessed is the one who has been found worthy of this gift and of this confidence and has seen this glorious vision with the eyes of the mind and heard with the ears of the heart the subtle sound that, from the state of serenity, is revealed to a spiritual person.[33]

Juan de la Cruz *1542–1591*

Human knowledge is not sufficient to comprehend it, nor human experience to describe it, because only one who has passed through it will be able to feel it, though not to tell it.

I entered I knew not where and remained there not knowing, passing beyond all knowledge.

I didn't know where I had entered but when I found I was there, without knowing where I was I learned many deep things; I can't say what I perceived because I remained unknowing, passing beyond all knowledge.

And so my soul was gifted with an understanding without understanding, passing beyond all knowledge.[34]

Jilani *1077–1166*

You do the giving up; he will do the giving.

Lock the door of your heart and make everything despair of getting inside. Then let in the remembrance of the Lord of Truth – and nothing else.

Do not allow your lower self to rear its head. Either you ride it, or it will ride you.[35]

Donkey mind ~ A story *Contemporary*

A man was trying to get his donkey to go across a stream. He pushed and he pulled, he threatened and he shouted – to no avail. The donkey wouldn't move.

His friend was watching and said, "Why don't you try doing it with love?"

So the man hugged the donkey, spoke lovingly, caressed it – but the donkey still wouldn't move.

Finally, in frustration he said to the friend, "Well, you do it then!"

The friend pulled a piece of 2x4 from the donkey's load and whacked the donkey over the head with it, then gently led the donkey across the stream.

"You call that love?" the man exclaimed.

The friend answered: "Well, first I had to get its attention!"[36]

Kabir

1398–1518

The Creator is everywhere,
In every thing,
But it's so hard for me to find him.
I haven't come across anybody
Who knows the secret,
So I'm wandering through this forest
Alone – wandering, mad from longing,
Absorbed inside.

I haven't been able to solve the mystery
So my body goes on suffering,
Self-afflicted.
I'm so restless for your darshan
But you don't let me see you.
My eyes want just one thing –
They're begging you.

He showed me!
He showed me how to see
With soul's hearing and seeing:
Finally body and mind are at peace –
The light! I saw the radiance
Of the one who holds my heart: Beloved!
Kabir has been singing his praises
Ever since.[37]

Abu Sa'id Ibn Abi'l Khayr *967–1049*

Spiritual hunger is a living, radiant fire put by God into the hearts of his servants so their ego can be burned; when it has been burned, this fire then becomes the fire of longing, which never dies, neither in this world nor the next.

There is no quicker way to God than spiritual hunger; if it travels through solid rock, water gushes forth. Spiritual hunger is essential for seekers; it is the showering of God's mercy on them.[38]

Plato *424–347* BCE

Imagine that one of the lifelong prisoners in an underground cavern is freed from his fetters and compelled to stand up suddenly and turn his head around and walk and lift up his eyes to the light; and in doing all this he feels pain, and because of the dazzle and glitter of the light is unable to discern the objects whose shadows he formerly saw.

And if someone should drag him from there by force up the ascent, which is rough and steep, and not let him go until he had drawn him out into the light of the sun, do you not think he would find it painful to be dragged along in this way, and that he would resist it, and when he came out into the light, his eyes would be so filled with its rays that he would not be able to see even one of the things we call real?

There would be a need of adjustment, of getting used to it, to enable him to see the things higher up. And at first he would most easily discern the shadows; and after that the likenesses or reflections in water of men and other things; and later, the things themselves; and from these he would go on to contemplate the appearances in the heavens and heaven itself – more easily by night, looking at the light of the stars and the moon, than by day, looking at the sun and the sun's light.

Finally, I suppose, he would be able to look at the sun itself and see its true nature – not by reflections in water or by an imaginary image of it in an alien setting, but in and by itself in its own place.[39]

Shams ad-Din Lahiji *1426–1506*

At the beginning of my mystical search, I knew nothing and so attached myself to the Imam Sayyed Mohammed Nurbaksh. During my second retreat of forty days, I saw the imam in a dream and he asked me, "Can you get up and give your place to someone else?" When I woke up, I thought that since I had made hardly any progress, this dream meant I should give my place to someone else who could benefit more from the master's presence.

That evening, I told my dream to the sheikh and what I had deduced from it. He said to me, "The real interpretation of your dream is this: you must forget your self and 'give up your place' to the supreme reality."

These words, which provoked a pain in my heart, marked the beginning of my spiritual evolution.[40]

Mundaka Upanishad *650–400* BCE

Two birds, mirror images of each other, inseparable friends, perch on a tree. One bird eats the fruits, the bitter and the sweet; the other bird watches, watches without eating, both birds clinging to the self-same hollow in the same tree – one suffering, engulfed by his impotence.

But as he watches the watching bird, the adorable one, and sees the sweet bitter glory as his own, he rises, free from grief.

Two birds, mirror images, inseparable friends, perched on a tree.[41]

Tulsi of Hathras

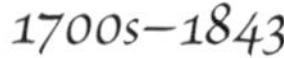

1700s–1843

Listen, Taqi, do not –
Under any circumstance –
Go searching outside:
Inside yourself is where you'll see
In all his radiant glory
The one who holds your heart.

In the pupil is the sesame seed:
Inside the sesame, it's full to the brim
With the secret that unravels the whole.
Look just a little beyond this black curtain –
That's where the fourteen realms
Will definitely be revealed to you.

Don't be careless –
Look with attention, stay alert:
And listen!
As you reach the first region
You'll hear a sound calling out to you.
This call has always been there,
Inviting you to see the Friend.

Meeting the Friend is not difficult;
What's hard, Taqi, is that it's hard
To see.
Without the grace of a master
Who has arrived,
The path to liberation is far off –
So how will you ever see beyond it?[42]

Eckhart *1250s–1329*

You need not look for God either here or there. He is no farther away than the door of your heart: there he stands waiting till he finds you ready to open the door and let him enter.

No need for you to call him from afar. He is waiting more impatiently than you for the door to be opened. He wants you a thousand times more urgently than you want him. There is only one thing you must do: open and let him enter.

No one has ever longed so much for anything as God is longing to bring man to him. God is so close to us, but we are distant and turned away from him. God is within, we are without; God is at home with us, we are strangers to ourselves.[43]

Chuang-tse *400s BCE*

Lao-tse tells a disciple:

If your obstructions are on the outside, do not attempt to grasp them one by one and thrust them away. Impossible! Learn to ignore them.

If they are within yourself, you cannot destroy them piecemeal but you can refuse to let them take effect.

If they are both inside and outside, do not try to hold on to Tao – just hope that Tao will keep hold of you![44]

Aurobindo *1872–1950*

The mind is a thing that dwells in diffusion, in succession; it can only concentrate on one thing at a time, and when not concentrated runs from one thing to another very much at random.

The first step in concentration must be always to accustom the discursive mind to a settled unwavering pursuit of a single course of connected thought on a single subject, and this it must do undistracted by all lures and alien calls on its attention.

Such concentration is common enough in our ordinary life, but it becomes more difficult when we have to do it inwardly without any outward object or action on which to keep the mind; yet this inward concentration is what the seeker of knowledge must effect.

To quiet the surface mind and begin to live within is the object of this concentration.[45]

Eugen Herrigel *1884–1955*

In the 1920s Eugen Herrigel, a German professor of philosophy recently arrived in Japan, was having tea in a fifth-floor restaurant with Awa Kenzo, who was later to become his archery master.

As Awa Kenzo speaks, Herrigel suddenly hears a low rumbling and feels a gentle heaving under his feet. The whole building is swaying and creaking, objects crashing, people calling out in alarm. The numerous guests, Europeans mostly, jump up from their tables and rush for the door to the corridor, heading for the stairs.

Like everybody else, Herrigel jumps up in order to run for safety, turning to his companion to urge him to hurry up. But Awa Kenzo is sitting there unmoved, hands folded, eyes nearly closed, as though nothing concerns him. Not like someone who hangs back irresolutely or who has not made up his mind, but like someone who, without fuss, is doing something – or not-doing something – perfectly naturally.

The sight is so astounding and has such a sobering effect that Herrigel can't move; he remains standing beside him. After a while he sits back down, gazing at Awa Kenzo without any thought of what it means or whether it is wise to remain. He feels spellbound, as though nothing can harm him.

The earthquake goes on for a fairly long time and Awa Kenzo continues the not-doing. When the earthquake subsides, to Herrigel's astonishment Awa Kenzo resumes the conversation calmly at the exact point where he had broken off. Herrigel, his whole body still chilled with terror, can only wonder what had held him in place, why he had not run away.

No satisfactory answers.

A few days later he learns that Awa Kenzo is a Zen Buddhist; his state of extreme concentration was such that he had become "unassailable."

This was the beginning of Herrigel's intense apprenticeship under an extraordinary master of archery.[46]

Farid 1173–1265

Axe on shoulder, waterpot on head,
The blacksmith is off to the forest or the pool.
Says Farid, All I want is my Beloved –
All you want is hot charcoal!

Farid, it's difficult being a beggar at the door
If you're travelling the worldly road.
The bundle on your back –
You're the one who tied the knot and lifted it up.
Where can you go to get rid of it now?

Farid, you've wasted the whole day
Wandering around,
And the night you've wasted asleep.
When God asks for your account, he'll say:
What did you come to the world for?[47]

Shams *1184–1247*

With all the effort you invest in discussing the way to God, it seems as if you wish to walk this road through knowledge! On this path, it is necessary to make the effort and endeavour to tread it.

Now words and talk should be put into action, not actions into words. Then you will understand that peace lies within the dervish.[48]

Yellow ribbons ~ A story *Traditional*

A young man feels cramped at home, angry because his parents are not providing what he wants, and tired of rural life and the day-in day-out routine on the farm. All he can think of is the excitement and adventure of setting out to explore the world. His parents try to dissuade him, telling him what the outside world is like, but he sets out anyway to make a living on his own.

Sometime after he leaves home, the Depression sets in and he can't get one square meal a day. He thinks to himself, "As long as I was with my parents, I had a roof over my head and food to eat. What has independence given me?"

He feels guilty, wondering whether his parents will take him back. So he writes asking for their forgiveness. He says, "I will be coming, but I feel bad. You are welcome to close the doors on me, but in case there is love in your heart and you forgive me, will you tie a yellow ribbon on the tree by the railway tracks? I will see it when I pass on the train and it will let me know whether you have forgiven me and want me back."

On the train he is so anxious, he knows he won't dare look at the tree. So he turns to one of the passengers, an elderly gentleman, and says: "After this bridge we'll pass a farm. Please tell me if there's a yellow ribbon on the tree by the railway tracks..."

The older man looks out of the window and says, "There's not one yellow ribbon – the whole tree is covered in them!"

Where there is love and dedication, the question of forgiveness does not arise: there is nothing to forgive.[49]

Pema Chödrön *1936–*

We can aspire to be kind right in the moment, to relax and open our heart and mind to what is in front of us right in the moment.

Now is the time. If there's any possibility for enlightenment, it's right now, not at some future time. Now is the time. Now is the only time.

When we realize that the path is the goal, there's a sense of workability. Trungpa Rinpoche said, "Whatever occurs in the confused mind is regarded as the path. Everything is workable. It is a fearless proclamation, the lion's roar."[50]

Coventry Patmore *1823–1896*

Shall I, a gnat which dances in Thy ray,
Dare to be reverent?[51]

Guru Arjan

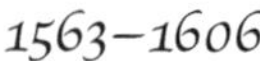

1563–1606

Through simran of the Lord
Our purpose is accomplished.
No more mourning!
Through that song of the Lord, the Word
Heard through simran, we merge back
Into Tranquillity: the soul's natural state.

Simran lets us sit unmoving:
The lotus blooms,
You hear a music no one plays.
This happiness of the Lord's simran –
It's unending, beyond limits!
People blessed with the grace of the Lord
Do simran. Nanak, it's with them
I seek refuge.[52]

Laurent de la résurrection

1614–1691

There is no mode of life in the world more pleasing and more full of delight than continual conversation with God. Only those who practise and experience it can understand it.

The time of work does not with me differ from the time of prayer, and in the agitation of my kitchen, while several people are calling out to me, asking for different things at the same time, I possess God in as great tranquillity as if I were upon my knees at the blessed sacrament.[53]

Nancy Pope Mayorga 1904–1983

The change of character which comes about through the struggle to practice the presence of God is both a means and a result.

You are offered the bait of delight. You taste it and it is withdrawn. Then with great care you watch yourself to see what are the most propitious moments and states of mind for this delight to reappear. You try not to let yourself get excited in your daily activities, either pleasurably or unpleasurably, because then at the time of meditation your mind will not be still enough for your spirit to feel that presence. You plan your day with careful economy so as to allow the greatest amount of free time possible for meditation.

Your whole life becomes a conspiracy with yourself to escape into God. And yet when escape is not possible, you cannot afford to allow yourself the least impatience, because impatience, too, defeats your end.

So you see yourself slowly becoming quiet, calm, patient and aloof, and you wonder at yourself, and you wonder with great and secret joy. Because all this seems infinitely right, exactly what you were made for. And there is contentment in your heart, so deep as to be unruffled by surface annoyances.[54]

The modern disciple ~ A story *Contemporary*

A teacher and his disciple were living in a forest. It started raining and the roof was leaking. The teacher said, "Why don't you take care of it." The disciple thought, If I go up on the roof, I'll get wet and perhaps slip down – so he humbly said: "It's not possible for me to be above and for you to be below me." So the teacher went up and mended the roof.

Then the teacher said, "Go out and get firewood to make our food." The disciple thought, It's cold out there, and there are wild animals – so he humbly said: "I wouldn't dream of turning my back on you!" So the teacher went out, collected firewood and prepared the meal.

Finally the teacher said, "Come and eat." The disciple dropped down on his knees and stretched out face down on the floor, in submission at the teacher's feet. He said, "I'm feeling very sad: twice I've disobeyed you. But now this third time, I promise I'll obey you absolutely, dear master!"[55]

The Buddha *563–485 BCE*

If a man were to conquer on the battlefield a thousand times a thousand men, and another conquer one, himself, he indeed is the greatest of conquerors. Be victorious over yourself and not over others![56]

Paltu

1700s–1800s

There was this other Paltu.
I was given the gift of devotion
Because they thought I was he.
I caught the Name he was supposed to get –
Paltu's devotion was given to me.

I found it lying there:
Somebody had dropped this incredible wealth.
I picked it up casually,
Closed my hands over it,
Hid it away.

It was fated otherwise
But somehow it got mixed in with my karmas.
I was the only one who knew –
Nobody else had any idea.

Eventually they found out.
They thought about it
But didn't take it back.
That's the way of the rich –
If they make a blunder, they can afford to let it go.

Paltu, I am a no-good.
God made a mistake.
There was this other Paltu –
He gave me devotion
Because he thought I was he.[57]

Dov Baer — *1700–1772*

I found a light in a closet; all I did was open the door.[58]

Hadith Qudsi — *600s*

The heavens and the earth do not contain Me, but the humble heart of My servant contains Me.[59]

The oyster and the pearl ~ A story — *1200s*

A pearl was in an oyster and this oyster was travelling the world observing other oysters. Though none of the others had a pearl, they were all telling the story of the oyster and the pearl. This oyster joined them in reciting the tales.

When the other oysters asked him "Do you have that pearl? We only hear stories about it", he answered: "I swear that I too only hear about it as you do."

"O you trickster and deceiver," they would say, "you have that pearl but are misleading us," and he would say, "No, I swear I do not."

He kept moving on in the world in the same fashion until one day he came across a unique jeweller who possessed the necessary qualifications to receive the pearl.

If you call this one an oyster, then do not also call the others oysters. How can an oyster within whom the pearl of God's mysteries has formed be addressed by the same name as a piece of broken clay?[60]

The Mother *1878–1973*

As long as the mind is convinced that it is the summit of human consciousness, that there is nothing beyond and above it, it takes its own functioning to be perfect and is fully satisfied with the progress it can make within the limits of this functioning.

What obstinate resistance in this lower nature, what blind and stupid attachment to the animal ways of being, what a refusal to liberate oneself!

When you open to the Spirit within you, it brings you a first foretaste of that higher life that alone is worth living; then comes the will to rise to that, the hope of reaching it, the certainty that this is possible; and finally the strength to make the necessary effort and the resolution to go to the very end.

First one must wake up, then one can conquer.[61]

PERSPECTIVE

The mystics explain that the primary challenge on the path is our mind, the ego. We cannot permanently subdue, suppress or kill off what Soami Ji of Agra calls "this restless mind that never keeps still." We need to come to terms with it, persuade it to work with us, persist as best we can when it doesn't, and be prepared for the long haul: our mind is unlikely to permanently turn inward overnight. As Paltu suggests, all of us are "no-goods." The task is to go on showing up every day, regardless.

The spiritual path may be about love, grace and joy – but the initial stages require persistent and regular practice. One needs to accept what is and be willing to keep on focusing and re-focusing inwardly. At some point the attention begins to let go of worldly thoughts and attachments and becomes aware of another attraction – the beginnings of what the mystics describe as the sweetness and fascination of what lies within.

Mystics say the mind is a lover of pleasure. It is restless and scattered because it is always searching outside in the world for new pleasures, never satisfied for long. Mind is afraid of the unknown, lacks self-control and is deluged by the senses; it automatically becomes tied to any people, places and things it desires.

Constantly distracted by our mind, says Farid, the danger is that we spend our whole life involved in the outer world and never discover the inner one – which is our spiritual purpose and the reason we came to the world. As disciples, the challenge is to use the spiritual practice to calm, focus and purify the mind – and to interact in the world with kindness, patience and respect.

Soami Ji, Guru Arjan and other mystics say that the mind is transformed and comes under control by merging our consciousness in the pure spiritual essence, Shabd – sometimes called Tranquillity, the Eternal Sound, the Great Mystery. Hearing that inner sound and seeing its projection, the light form of the teacher, are said to be the key to a disciple's spiritual evolution. Why? Perhaps because all barriers to realization – mind, ego, desire and all our personas and coverings – are annihilated in the enchantment of that inner Presence.

Spirit, Truth, Shabd, is already within us – it is the essence of our own being – but as Kabir says, we have lost the secret to hearing and seeing it. Every mystic says that longing plays a role here… finding a guide to show us the practice… living a way of life based on humane behaviour… and giving time and effort every day to turning the attention inwards toward the inner way.

The songpoems describe ultimate realization as becoming one with the ocean of Spirit, the eternal essence. But they say the turning point in a disciple's journey is seeing the radiant or light form of the teacher. Gazing inside, contemplating "the one who holds your heart," as Tulsi of Hathras and Kabir put it, is the magnificent stage when the teacher allows the student to see that constant companion, the one who has invisibly been there all along – the inner guide.

Longing for that Presence, seeing it and missing it, is the push-pull ascent in the game of love that culminates in union – oneness with the ultimate, the source.

The Master

The spiritual teacher –
the guide and guardian on the inner way
and the physical link with the spiritual mysteries.
While alive he accepts responsibility
for a seeker's return
to full consciousness or realization
and gives the gift of initiation
into the inner practice;
he does not leave the disciple
until the goal is reached.

1. **Soami Ji of Agra**
   Show me your real form! p.62
   guru mohé apana roop dikhaao

   Soami Ji of Agra
   My form is strange and extraordinary
   dékh pyaaré mai~ samjhaa'oo~

   - Mechthild von Magdeburg: All that Mine is
   - Rabindranath Tagore: The beggar
   - Shams: The price I pay

2. **Nanak**
   What is the root? p.66
   kavan/u mool/u kavan/u mat/i véla

   - John: In the beginning was the Word
   - Give what is yours ~ A story

3. **Dadu**
   Hey, disciple, learn to recognize p.69
   niranjan jogi jaani lé chéla

   - *Chaandogya Upanishad:* You are that!
   - Catarina Benincasa of Siena: I am He who is
   - Aurobindo: The supreme sign of a master
   - Bonaventura: I became a visible man

4. **Ravidas**
What shows the goodness of a saint? p.73
ravidaas so'i saadhoo bhalo
- Ramon Lull: The lover wept
- Bukhara and the drunkard ~ A story

5. **Tulsi of Hathras**
Go on watching! p.75
aré ai taqi takté raho
- *Joseph and Aseneth*: The man of light
- Ba'al Shem Tov: Searching within
- Fakhr ad-Din Araqi: In the light I praised you

6. **Paltu**
Soothing as sandalwood, serene as the moon p.75
seetal chandan chandrama
- What do you see in me? ~ A story
- Chuang-tse: The man of Tao
- Nancy Pope Mayorga: Interview with her teacher

Perspective p.82

Soami Ji of Agra

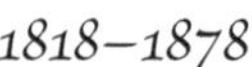

1818–1878

Dear Master, show me your real form!
You put on this form and all its qualities
To take people across to liberation,
But your real form is beyond reach,
Limitless, no boundaries –
Show me that one now!
Once I've seen it, I'll sit quiet, in bliss.
Oh yes – and grant me the gift of fearlessness!

I love this form, too –
It's through this one I learned about that one.
Without this form, the job cannot be done –
How else would you reveal the other one?
So all praise to this one,
But show me that one, too –
The one you assume eternally
Even as you awaken souls here.
It's from you I learned this secret –
You're always singing about the Surat Shabd path.

The Shabd form, your real form,
Let my soul merge in it now!
I'm always afraid of death and suffering –
Make me fearless, lift me to liberation!

Compassionate to the wretched,
Benefactor to the soul,
Fulfil my life's purpose, Radha Soami,
Lord of my soul!

Listen, dear one, I'll explain to you:
My form is strange and extraordinary.
Nobody can see it unless I help them to.
So do your practice – overcome the mind
And close the doors of the senses.
Lift up your attention, soar to the sky
Of Trikuti, cross over the peak of Sunn.

I'll show you my form as Sat Purush, the True Being,
And I'll show you the Unseeable, Alakh,
And the Unreachable, Agam.
Beyond all these is Radha Soami, Lord of the soul –
And that is my own real form.

Be patient, keep the company of the true,
And by grace you'll be prepared
And put right. I won't give up
Until I've shown you that form –

Why be in such a hurry, calling out like this?
I've taken all your worries into my heart
So you can remain free from anxiety
And nurture my love in yours.

Sustained by understanding and conviction,
Let go of doubts, hold on to love.
I myself will make sure your practice gets done!
I will take you back to the court of the Lord
From where everything began.
Radha Soami has spoken for you to hear:
It will all take place exactly as and when
His sweet will ordains.[62]

Mechthild von Magdeburg *1207–1294*

If you would have all that Mine is, you must give me all that yours is.

If you have the weights, I have the gold.[63]

Rabindranath Tagore *1861–1941*

I had gone a-begging from door to door in the village path, when thy golden chariot appeared in the distance like a gorgeous dream and I wondered who was this King of all kings!

My hopes rose high and methought my evil days were at an end, and I stood waiting for alms to be given unasked and for wealth scattered on all sides in the dust.

Thy chariot stopped where I stood. Thy glance fell on me and thou camest down with a smile. I felt that the luck of my life had come at last. Then of a sudden thou didst hold out thy right hand and say "What hast thou to give to me?"

Ah, what a kingly jest was it to open thy palm to a beggar to beg! I was confused and stood undecided, and then from my wallet I slowly took out the least little grain of wheat and gave it to thee.

But how great my surprise when at the day's end I emptied my bag on the floor to find a least little grain of gold among the poor heap. I bitterly wept and wished that I had had the heart to give thee my all.[64]

Shams *1184–1247*

I am riding with a hundred horses and I am focused on you. You get busy somewhere else. You can, but I cannot. I am focused on you with full attention. Having all of me involved with all of you is the price I pay for giving all of me to all of you.[65]

Nanak

1469–1539

A group of venerable yogis, high in the Himalayas,
question the young stranger, Nanak:
What is the root?
What is the path of the time?
Who is your master –
Whose disciple are you?
What recitation do you do
To remain detached?

We have spoken, Nanak –
Hear it well, my boy!
Explain to us this conundrum:
How can a word take you across
The ocean of existence?

Nanak answers:
The beginning was from air.
The path of the time
Is the path of the true masters.
Shabd is the master –
Consciousness merged in Sound
Is the disciple.
I remain detached by repeating
The unspoken recitation.

Says Nanak, Throughout the ages
The master is the Lord of the world:
Whoever meditates on the conundrum
Of the one Word,
Through the gurmukh
Is protected from the fire of ego.[66]

John *100s*

In the beginning was the Word, and the Word was with God, and the Word was God; it was in the beginning with God. All things came into being because of it, and without it not even one thing was made manifest of all that emerged.

In it was life – and the life was the light for human beings. The light shines in the darkness, and the darkness perceived it not.

There was a man, sent as a messenger from very close to God; his name was John. He came as a witness to testify about the light, that all might believe by means of him. He was not the light, but was sent that he might bear witness of the light.

True was the light: it lights up every person who comes into the world. It was in the world, and the world was made manifest through it – and the world had no experience of it!

He came unto his own, and his own received him not.[67]

Give what is yours ~ A story *1500s*

For twenty years or so, the mystic Nanak travelled all over India and beyond. He went on foot, sometimes dressed as a pilgrim, sometimes as an ascetic – going as far as Assam in the east and Saudi Arabia in the west, Tibet in the far north and Sri Lanka in the far south. Nanak met with hundreds of people, speaking about Shabd and Naam with anybody who was interested, shaking up people's fixed beliefs, and awakening hearts and minds among the many who saw and heard him.

In Sri Lanka the king Shivnabh heard much from his courtiers about the teacher Nanak and eventually came to visit him. They talked for a while, and then the king fell at Nanak's feet, saying: "I want to give you something! Let me give you all my jewels."

But Nanak said, "They are not yours to give. They belong to the kingdom."

The king said, "I'll give you my kingdom."

Nanak replied: "It is not yours to give. It belongs to your son, who will inherit it as you inherited it from your father."

"Then I'll give you my body," said the king.

But Nanak told him: "It is not yours either. One day you will die and your body will be cremated."

"So what can I give?" asked the king.

"Everything has been given to you by God, so give me the one thing you have created: your ego. Give me your 'I'."[68]

Dadu

1544–1603

Hey, disciple, learn to recognize
The jogi who has no stain!

He permeates all, yet lives alone.
He has no begging bowl, no bag or staff.
He doesn't live in a mud hut,
He takes money from no one.

He doesn't blow a horn,
He adopts no yogic postures.
He belongs to no group,
He doesn't brag about lineage.

He doesn't smear his body with ashes
Nor wear saffron robes.
No matted ascetic's hair,
No counted repetitions.

No prayer mat, no daily rounds.
No pilgrimages, no fasting, no jungle dwelling.
No begging, no feasting, no worldly expectations.

Immortal the guru, indestructible the jogi!
Says Dadu: His disciples have no self-control –
Without restraint they indulge in drinking
Elixir.[69]

Chaandogya Upanishad *650–400* BCE

"Please sir, instruct me further."

"So be it, my son. Throw this salt into water and come back to me in the morning."

Svetaketu did as he was told.

Uddaalaka said, "Take out the salt you put into the water yesterday evening."

Svetaketu felt around but could not find it: "All the salt has dissolved."

"Taste the water at the near side. How is it?"

"Like salt."

"And in the middle?"

"Like salt."

"And at the far side?"

"Like salt."

"Now you have tasted it, come to me."

Svetaketu came to him and said, "It is all the same."

Uddaalaka explained: "You do not perceive it, but *sat*, 'being', is right here. Everything, this whole world, has that subtle essence as soul. That essence is being – *sat*, what is real or true; it is *aatman*, soul; and, O Svetaketu, it is you: You are that!"[70]

Catarina Benincasa of Siena 1347–1380

Do you know, daughter, who you are and who I am? If you know these two things, you will be blessed. You are she who is not, whereas I am He who is.[71]

Aurobindo 1872–1950

Teaching, example, influence – these are the three instruments of the guru. But the wise teacher will not seek to impose himself or his opinions on the passive acceptance of the receptive mind; he will throw in only what is productive and sure as a seed that will grow under the divine fostering within.

He will seek to awaken the faculties and the experiences by a natural process and free expansion. He will give a method as an aid, as a usable device, not as an imperative formula or a fixed routine. And he will be on his guard against any turning of the means into a limitation, against the mechanizing of process.

His whole business is to awaken the divine light and set working the divine force of which he himself is only a means and an aid, a body or a channel.

Example is more powerful than instruction; but it is not the example of the outward acts nor that of the personal character that are of most importance. These have their place and their utility; but what will most stimulate aspiration in others is the central fact of the divine realization within the teacher governing his whole life and inner state and all his activities.

This is the universal and essential element; the rest belongs to individual person and circumstance. It is the dynamic realization that the practitioner must feel and reproduce in himself according to his own nature; he need not strive after an imitation from outside, which may well be sterilizing rather than productive of right and natural fruits.

Influence is more important than example. Influence is not the outward authority of the teacher over his disciple, but the power of his contact, of his presence, of the nearness of his soul to the soul of another, infusing into it, even though in silence, that which he himself is and possesses.

This is the supreme sign of the master. For the greatest master is much less a teacher than a Presence pouring the divine consciousness and its constituting light and power and purity and bliss into all who are receptive around him.

His work, if he has one, is a trust from above, he himself a channel, a vessel or a representative. He is a man helping his brothers, a child leading children, a light kindling other lights, an awakened soul awakening souls, at highest a power or presence of the divine calling to him other powers of the divine.[72]

Bonaventura *1221–1274*

I became a visible man so that on seeing me you might love me, the One whom in my divinity you could not see and did not love. I gave myself to you; give yourself to me.[73]

Ravidas

1414–1540

Ravidas, what shows the goodness of a saint?
He knows the pain of others –
Just seeing their pain
Makes him constantly restless.

Ravidas, what shows the goodness of a saint?
He's involved in helping others –
He goes into action, doing what he talks about
Without drawing attention to himself.

I amassed a lot of capital
In the company of saints
And managed to buy the Thing –
The priceless goods. Ravidas,
I've loaded up my bullock with Tranquillity
And I'm off to pay any price
For the Beloved![74]

Ramon Lull *1233–1315*

The lover wept and called upon his Beloved, until the Beloved came down from the heights of heaven; and he came down to earth to weep and suffer and die for the sake of love, and to teach people how to know and love and praise his Name.[75]

Bukhara and the drunkard ~ A story *1400s*

Long before he set out in search of a spiritual teacher, the king of Bukhara was a seeker and a man of compassion. He used to leave his palace at night disguised as an ordinary citizen so he could go among his people, listening to them, observing them, interacting and talking with them – all to find out how he could best help and encourage them.

One evening he came across a drunkard lying unconscious in the gutter that ran down the middle of the roadway. The muck and filth of the neighbourhood flowed into the man's open mouth and had soaked his ragged clothing. Everybody detoured around him; he was wet and dirty, he stank, and he was oblivious.

The king pulled him to the side of the road, cleaned his mouth, face and hair with water from a nearby well, and then sat gently cushioning his head in his lap and fanning him with his hand to keep the flies away.

Eventually the man's eyes fluttered open a crack and he suddenly became conscious. Gazing alert and startled into the eyes of his rescuer, he wept. "Here I am, a filthy drunkard, and I wake up in the lap of my king!"[76]

Tulsi of Hathras

1700s–1843

Come on, Taqi: Go on watching!
The master is offering you his hand –
Wide open, five fingers welcoming:
Don't become stupefied and give up
If you're longing to behold the Beloved
In all his radiant splendour!

His grace will be with you
All the way to the court and his throne:
No fear or danger can follow you.
You are to go straight there –
That is the master's decree.

Mansur, Sarmad, Bu Ali, Shams, Maulana –
They all reached the ultimate
Through this same path,
Once it strengthened their hearts
With unshakeable resolve.

The destination of the path is love!
Yet reaching there is not difficult:
The dissolver of difficulties is nearby –
He has already given you his hand.

Says Tulsi: Listen, Taqi, the inner secret
Is extraordinary, unexpected.
Guard it carefully – it will give you conviction
And direct you upwards.

If you're longing to behold the Beloved,
Go on watching, Taqi – go on watching![77]

Joseph and Aseneth ~ A story *200s*

And as Aseneth went on gazing, behold, the heaven near the morning star opened and a great and ineffable light appeared. And when Aseneth saw it she fell on her face upon the ashes; and there came to her from heaven a man of light, rays radiating from him. And he stood by her head and called to her, saying, "Aseneth, arise."

And Aseneth raised her head and looked up and saw a man, the image of Joseph in every respect, with a robe and a crown and a royal staff. But his face was like lightning and his eyes were like sunshine and the hairs of his head like flames of fire. And his hands and his feet were like iron shining from a furnace, with sparks emanating from his hands and from his feet.[78]

Ba'al Shem Tov *1698–1760*

There was once a wise and great king who did everything through illusion, constructing imaginary walls, towers, gates and palaces. And he commanded the people to come to him through the gates and the towers, and instructed that royal treasures be scattered at each and every gate and in all the palatial rooms.

And there were some people who came to one of the outer gates and filled their pockets with metal coins and went away content. Others ventured to one of the inner gates and filled their pockets with semi-precious stones, copper and silver, and went away content. A few entered the towers and rooms of the illusory palaces and filled sacks with jewels and gold, and went away content.

Only one person ignored the treasures and went on searching and searching, never stopping at the gates or in any of the vast rooms, climbing to the tops of the towers, looking always for just one thing: the king.

And when at last he found him, he saw there was no barrier separating him from his beloved father, for it was all an illusion.[79]

Fakhr ad-Din Araqi *1213–1289*

In the light I praised you
  and never knew it.
In the dark I slept with you
  and never knew it.
I always thought that I was me,
But no, I was you
  and never knew it.[80]

Paltu

1700s–1800s

Soothing as sandalwood, serene as the moon:
The saint is like that. Soothing, serene,
He puts out the burning of the world.
If anyone comes to him on fire, all they need
Is the sweetness of his face, the sound of his words.

His charm, patience, humility, forgiveness –
They cannot be described.
Soft as a lotus petal,
His gentle voice and loving words
Melt stone, turn granite into water!

The way he lives, the way he walks,
the way he smiles,
Bring fragrance to the path of enlightenment.
When we gaze, lost in the eyes of a saint,
All burning is extinguished – body, mind, soul.
Paltu, even the hunger of desire is snuffed out.

Soothing as sandalwood, serene as the moon:
The saint is like that.[81]

What do you see in me? ~ A story *1000s*

The famous eleventh-century Chinese scholar and poet Su Dong Po was visiting Fo Yin, a Buddhist monk. Su Dong Po joined Fo Yin in meditation.

After a while Su Dong Po opened his eyes and asked the monk, "What do you see in me when I am meditating?"

The monk nodded in approval and said, "You look like a stately Buddha!"

Su Dong Po was very happy with this response.

A little later the monk asked Su Dong Po, "What do you see in me when I am meditating?"

Su Dong Po immediately replied: "You look like a pile of dung!"

The monk smiled and said nothing. Su Dong Po was delighted, thinking he had scored a winning point over the monk.

He returned home in a good mood and told his sister, Su Xiaomei, all about it. To his surprise, she laughed at him.

"Brother, you are a fool. The monk Fo Yin sees you as a Buddha because he sees everything as the Buddha – he has the Buddha's heart and the Buddha's eyes. You see the monk Fo Yin as dung because you see everything as dung. I'm sorry to say it, brother, but your words show you have a heart of dung and eyes of dung."[82]

Chuang-tse 400s BCE

The man in whom Tao acts without impediment harms no other being by his actions, yet he does not know himself to be "kind," to be "gentle."

The man in whom Tao acts without impediment does not bother with his own interests and does not despise others who do. He does not struggle to make money and does not make a virtue of poverty. He goes his way without relying on others and does not pride himself on walking alone. While he does not follow the crowd, he won't complain of those who do. Rank and reward make no appeal to him; disgrace and shame do not deter him. He is not always looking for right and wrong, always deciding Yes or No.

The ancients said, therefore:

> The man of Tao
> Remains unknown.
> Perfect virtue
> Produces nothing:
> No-Self
> Is True-Self –
> And the greatest man
> Is Nobody.[83]

Nancy Pope Mayorga *1904–1983*

Swami Prabhavananda: Did I ever explain to you about mental worship?

Mayorga: No.

(How to explain what happened then? As he began to talk – simple things, looking at me with the deepest intensity – I felt a stillness in me that I had never felt before, that is past describing. Every atom of me was still and listening, held by his words and his look. Suspended. Breath and everything. And the beauty of what he was imparting to me, not alone in words, filled me with astonishment and bliss. He kept looking at me deeply, to make sure I understood, asking me if I understood. And if I had not been so transfixed, I would have wept for joy. And now, of course, the effect of those words has been tremendous. I have lived the past days in almost constant bliss, feeling the touch of God again and again, immobilized at times with joy. The strange mystery of that power. I want it for my own. Yes, I do. I aspire to that.)[84]

PERSPECTIVE

In the mystic tradition the spiritual teacher is the human link with the world of the inner mysteries. The living master is the way a seeker is given the gift of initiation into the subtle energy variously referred to as Spirit, the Way, the Word. And the true teacher is a constant guide on the inner path to realization of that mysterious power.

Nanak, Soami Ji of Agra, Kabir and so many other mystics say that Shabd (or Tao or Spirit or Word) is the master because that is the real form of a true teacher or fully realized person. In that form, says Dadu, he is immortal, indestructible.

The mystics also tell us that the real form of the ordinary person is not the physical body, the mind or the personality, but consciousness, or *surat* as it is called in the bhakti tradition. To know we have a form other than our present identity, this body-mind, they invite us to achieve, during this lifetime, liberation from the body and from the mind. As we emerge, we begin to know who we really are.

The masters come to the world as human beings in order to communicate with us. They assume a form we relate to, speak a language people understand, and lead a life as our contemporary in a world whose challenges they also deal with. But the mystic tradition indicates that their human form should not delude us into thinking they are merely human like the rest of us.

The bhakti mystics explain that people are drawn to the teacher to learn about their spiritual potential and how they can spiritually evolve. Day by day, through meditation, they establish a relationship with the eternal inner Presence, the Shabd or Sound. Ultimately, through love – longing, humility, séva and the meditation practice – they are purified and prepared for the merging of consciousness in that spiritual essence.

As for intimacy in relationship with the Beloved, it is oneness in Spirit or Shabd. It intensifies progressively as the disciple merges in higher levels of Shabd, culminating in union – total awakening and realization on all levels. And that is when the disciple comes to know who the master really is.

True spiritual teachers are motivated, as Ravidas says, by compassion, by knowing the pain of others – not by ego, desire, fame, power, money or greed. They cannot be recognized, says Dadu, by what they wear or how they live. Their spiritual practice is inner, unseen. Their great transformative role is in turning people into human beings – for once somebody is truly human, say the mystics, it is a short step to becoming divine.

The living masters themselves represent the human ideal. They show it is possible to live the teachings even under the stressful and sometimes overwhelming situations in today's world. In spite of their complex responsibilities and the numerous demands on their time, they are an unfailing embodiment of love, humour, equanimity and integrity. Simultaneously powerful and gentle, loving but firm, brilliant but unobtrusive, they encourage, they command, and they inspire.

The mystics admit, as Paltu says, that it is the teacher's physical presence in the disciple's life that brings "fragrance" to the path of enlightenment, making it possible to participate and persevere in the spiritual practice. His outer guidance and initiation are essential. His company is sustaining – inspiring, uplifting, energizing. And his constant presence in his inner radiant form is the "dissolver of difficulties," as Tulsi of Hathras puts it.

The master in his subtle form, magnetic and powerful, is the attractive force that gradually pulls the consciousness of the meditator inward and upward – supporting one's evolution towards realization of the inner mysteries.

The Mystery

The resonating and illuminating
inner Truth is not words
but the mysterious divine power within all of us
that manifests as inner sound and light.
We become attuned to its frequency
by the grace of a true teacher
through the practice of meditation
under his guidance, attention and care.

1. **Guru Arjan**
   Do just one thing p.88
   saajan sant karahu ihu kaam/u
   - Yannus Chrysostomos: Prayer of the heart
   - The rock ~ A story
   - *The Cloud of Unknowing:* What you would be
   - Aurobindo: Not speaking of inner experiences

2. **Paltu**
   They all talk about the Name of God p.91
   naam naam sab kahat hai~
   - Epictetus: Join me in this same song
   - Isaiah: Awake and sing
   - Yogananda: The greatest romance

3. **Tegh Bahadur**
   The Name p.94
   naam/u rahio saadhoo rahio
   - Pinhas of Korets: Prayer and God
   - François de Sales: Bring yourself back
   - The Mother: The reversal of consciousness
   - Chuang-tse: The empty boat

4. **Kabir**
Kabir, these two lines p.97
kabeer adhi saakh koᴛh granth ko jaan
- Zechariah: His Name
- Philo: Logos, food of the soul
- James: Doers of the Word
- Prabhavananda: The essentials
- *Sefer ha-Bahir*: I am the One

5. **Soami Ji of Agra**
Soul is playing inside on the swing p.99
ghaᴛ jhum rahi ab surat rangeeli
- Juan de la Cruz: Hidden treasure
- Jami: The tinkling of the bells
- Nancy Pope Mayorga: Holding what we have

6. **Mira**
I've got it! p.102
paayo ji mai~ to naam ratan dhan paayo
- True song ~ Iroquois legend
- *Book of Coming Forth into the Light*: God is a Spirit
- Jesus: The Spirit of Truth

Perspective p.107

Guru Arjan

1563–1606

Listen, saints,
Beloved friends of mine!
Do just one thing
And forget all other practices:
Repeat God's name.

Doing simran, simran,
Again and again, you'll find happiness.
By doing the repetition yourself
You'll inspire others to meditate, too.
Through love and devotion you'll go safely across –
Beyond this world of coming and going.

Without devotion, the human form
Is nothing but dust. Prosperity, happiness,
It's all in this treasure, the Name!
It gives even the drowning a place of rest
Because it puts an end to pain and suffering.

Says Nanak, Meditate on his Name –
It's the storehouse of excellence:
The Lord himself![85]

Yannus Chrysostomos *347–407*

It is possible to pray at all times, in all circumstances and in every place, and to rise easily from frequent vocal prayer to prayer of the mind, and from that to prayer of the heart, which opens up the kingdom of God within.[86]

The rock ~ A story *Traditional*

God instructs one of his devotees to push a huge rock, and to do this every day, at least once a day.

For thirty years the devotee pushes the rock every day. But finally he gives up: "What's the use? The rock hasn't moved an inch in all these years of pushing."

The next day God comes to him and asks, "Why have you stopped pushing?"

"Because I'll never be able to move the rock!"

"If I wanted to move the rock, I could do it in a moment. I want you to push it, that's all."

The devotee goes back to pushing the rock.[87]

The Cloud of Unknowing *1300s*

For it is not what you are or have been that God looks at with his merciful eyes, but what you would be.[88]

Aurobindo *1872–1950*

The usual rule given by yogis is that one should not speak of one's experience to others while the practice is going on, except of course the guru, because it wastes the experience.

It is safest not to speak of these experiences – except to a guru or to one who can help you.

The passing away of an experience as soon as it is spoken of is a frequent happening and for that reason many yogis recommend not speaking of what happens within you unless it is a thing of the past or a settled realization that nothing can take away – only long past experiences, and even that not too freely.[89]

Paltu

1700s–1800s

Naam, the Name –
They all talk about the Name of God
But none of them gets it.
None of them has found the Name –
Naam is something very different.
The person who kills expectations gets it.

You quieten the ego;
No consciousness remains in the body.
Inside the cave in the inner sky
You drink deep the cup of love.

Once you dye mind in love's colour,
Hunger and thirst are forgotten:
The five and the twenty-five –
The passions and our characteristics –
They all remain on this side,
And they run far away
From the company you keep!

Detached, inwardly alone,
That's when the melody speaks so sweetly.
What one hears cannot be expressed –
How can I possibly describe it?

Paltu, through the mercy of the master
We remain asleep to the world.

Naam, the Name –
They all talk about the Name of God
But none of them gets it.[90]

Epictetus — *55–135*

What else can I do, a lame old man, but sing hymns to God? If I were a nightingale, I would do the nightingale's part; if I were a swan, I would do as a swan. But now I am a rational creature who ought to praise God: this is my work. I do it, nor will I desert my post so long as I am allowed to keep it. And I exhort you to join me in this same song.[91]

Isaiah — *700s BCE*

Awake and sing, you that dwell in dust!

You shall have a song, as in the night
  when a holy solemnity is kept;
And gladness of heart, as when one goes with a flute
  to come into the mountain of the Lord,
  to the rock of Israel.
And the Lord shall cause his glorious voice to be heard.[92]

Yogananda *1893–1952*

The greatest romance is with the Infinite. You have no idea how beautiful life can be.

> Unattracted to the sensory world, the yogi experiences the ever-new joy of Being. His soul engaged in union with Spirit, he attains indestructible bliss.
>
> *Bhagavad Gita*, V:21

When you suddenly find God everywhere, when he comes and talks to you and guides you, the romance of divine love has begun.

Dive deep in the ocean of meditation. If you don't find the pearls of his presence, don't blame the ocean, blame your diving. Dive again and again until you find him.

Let no devotee miss his daily appointment with God. The mind may suggest the movies or some other distraction; but when the time comes for God each day, keep the sacred engagement. Otherwise you will be a long time finding him.[93]

Tegh Bahadur

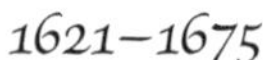

1621–1675

The Name,
The devotee,
Guru and God –
Just these last forever.

Yet how few in the world –
One in a million, Nanak –
Repeat the mantra of the master![94]

Pinhas of Korets

1726–1791

Prayer is not *to* God; prayer *is* God himself.[95]

François de Sales

1567–1622

Bring yourself back to the point quite gently. And even if you do nothing during the whole of your hour but bring your heart back a thousand times, though it went away every time you brought it back, your hour would be very well employed.[96]

The Mother *1878–1973*

To live the spiritual life, a reversal of consciousness is needed. To live the spiritual life is to open to another world within oneself – to reverse one's consciousness, as it were.

The ordinary human consciousness, even in the most developed, even in people of great talent and great understanding, is a movement turned outwards – all the energies directed outwards, the whole consciousness spread outwards. And if anything is turned inwards, it is very little, very rare, very fragmentary.

There is a difference between aspiration, even the straining of the highest most luminous mind, and realization, which is something that has been decided above from all time and is absolutely independent of all personal effort, of all gradation.

Don't you see, it is not bit by bit that one reaches realization; it is not by a small, constant, regular effort – it comes suddenly, established without one's knowing how or why... but all is changed.

Instead of being here, one is there; instead of seeing from outside and seeking to see within, one is inside. And the minute one is within, absolutely everything changes.

Once the reversal has taken place, you can glide into an external consciousness, not lose the ordinary contact with the things of life – but the internal consciousness remains, it never goes away. One no longer seeks, one sees. One no longer deduces, one knows. One no longer gropes, one walks straight to the goal.[97]

Chuang-tse *400s BCE*

The way to get clear of confusion and free of sorrow is to live with Tao in the land of the great Void.

If a man is crossing a river and an empty boat collides with his own skiff, even though he be a bad-tempered man he will not become very angry. But if he sees a man in the boat, he will shout at him to steer clear. If the shout is not heard, he will shout again, and yet again, and begin cursing. And all because there is somebody in the boat! Yet if the boat were empty, he would not be shouting, and not angry.

If you can empty your own boat, crossing the river of the world no one will oppose you, no one will seek to harm you. You will flow like Tao, unseen. You will go about like Life itself, with no name and no home.

Simple, without distinction. To all appearances, a fool. Steps leave no trace. You have no power. You achieve nothing, have no reputation. Since you judge no one, no one judges you.

Such is the perfect man: His boat is empty.[98]

Kabir 1398–1518

Kabir, these two lines
Sum up a thousand scriptures:

Naam is true, the world is false;
Recognize it through Surat Shabd –

The merging of consciousness
In Shabd, the Sound or Word.[99]

Zechariah 500s BCE

In that day shall the Lord be one, and his Name one.[100]

Philo 20 BCE–50 CE

Do you not see the food of the soul, what it is? It is the Logos of God, the Word, raining continuously like dew, embracing all the soul, suffering no portion to be without part of itself.

But this Logos is not apparent everywhere, but only in the person who is destitute of passions and vices; and it is subtle and delicate both to conceive and be conceived, surpassingly translucent and pure to behold.[101]

James *100s*

Become therefore doers of the Word, and not hearers only, deceiving yourselves.[102]

Prabhavananda *1893–1976*

Always I tell my disciples two things are needed – patience and perseverance.

One of the most important things is recollection. Try to remember God, always.[103]

Sefer ha-Bahir *1300s*

I am the One who planted this tree in order that all the world should delight in it. And in it I spread All. I call it *All* because all depend on it, all emanate from it, and all need it. To it they look, for it they wait, and from it souls fly in joy.

Alone was I when I made it. Let no angel rise above it and say, "I was before you." I was also alone when I spread out my earth, in which I planted and rooted this tree.

I made them rejoice together, and I rejoiced in them.[104]

Soami Ji of Agra 1818–1878

Soul is playing inside on the swing,
Overjoyed with laughter and love.
The veil between: she's thrown it far away –
She's heard the Shabd, the Word,
The melodious voice of the Beloved!

She turns inward from the eyes,
Thrusts her way through the sesame door
And sees the brilliant light of a dazzling flame.
Pounded with ringing reverberating sounds,
She dances in delight, lovely – his light! –
Soaring to the heights of Trikuti in ecstasy.

She swims in the stream of Sound,
Emerging clean, free at last of filth
And all those clinging characteristics.
She goes on alone to the lake of Maansarovar,
Withdrawn, one-pointed
In the mysterious attraction of the Word.

Rising higher still, she reaches the Great Darkness,
Caught up in extraordinary games unknown.
In moments she catches the Shabd of Satnaam,
Supreme sound of the true Name.
The vine of soul has climbed the Shabd tree –
She's put on the garland of the Ineffable Name![105]

Juan de la Cruz *1542–1591*

If you want to find a hidden treasure, you must enter the hiding place secretly; and once you have discovered it, you will also be hidden just as the treasure is hidden.

Your beloved Bridegroom is the treasure, and the field where the treasure is hidden is your soul.

So if you want to find him, forget everything else and hide in the secret inner chamber of your spirit. Closing the door behind you, pray there to your Father in secret.

Remaining hidden with him, you will experience him in hiding, you will love him and enjoy him in hiding – in a way that goes beyond language, beyond feeling: far beyond.[106]

Jami *1414–1492*

If you are not so fortunate as to join the caravan of the Beloved, at least enjoy listening in the early morning to the distant tinkling of the bells![107]

Nancy Pope Mayorga *1904–1983*

If I were to give one piece of advice to spiritual aspirants, it would be steadiness, regularity in practice. Gerald Heard used to meditate six hours a day "because," he said, "I don't want to lose what I have." I don't have what he has, but the little bit I have has to be held by practice.

I am adept – that is, I can quiet my mind to feel the contact with God. But I am not so adept that I don't notice the adverse effect of missing one day's practice. When I am sick, I mourn over my lost practice, and that seems to have somewhat the same effect as meditation because when I am well again, my first meditation period is one of tremendous, inexpressible joy. A return home. Relief and surrender and bliss.

Ah God! My beloved! Why don't you take me?[108]

Mira

1498–1573

I've got it!
I've got the treasure –
The jewel of the Name.

My master has given me
This Thing – it's priceless!
With such compassion and forgiveness
He has made me his own.

Now I've got the wealth
I lost so many lifetimes ago:
I'm free from everything
Tying me to this world!

What a gift –
It doesn't get spent,
Thieves can't steal it,
And it goes on increasing every day.

There's a boat of truth
And satguru is the boatman –
He came and sailed me across
The ocean of existence.

Mira's Lord, upholder of mountains,
I go from happiness to ecstasy
Just singing your praise:
I've got it, the jewel of the Name![109]

True song ~ Iroquois legend *Traditional*

The Creator, walking through the creation one day, saw all the birds gathered around the village of the people.

"Why are you here?" the Creator asked.

The birds answered, "We have watched the people working, playing, walking and praying. They sing as they do these things. It is so beautiful, we birds wish we could sing." For the birds at that time did not sing but only talked like the other animals.

"Gather tomorrow at noon, at the Council Rock in the clearing," said the Creator, "and I will tell you what I have decided."

So the birds gathered eagerly at the Council Rock and awaited the Creator.

The Creator came to them and told them, "Gather again at this Council Rock tomorrow before dawn. When the first rays of the sun touch the Council Rock, fly as high as you can. Each of you, when you have flown to your own greatest height, will find there a song. This will be only for you – your song, to keep and to sing forever."

The birds gathered next morning when it was still dark. They talked excitedly among themselves. They could hardly wait for the sun to rise – all except little Hermit Thrush. Hermit Thrush was a shy bird, timid and quiet. It found itself next to the great Eagle, Stagwi'ah, who was strong of talon and wing, it is true, but was also strong of heart, and so could be kind and gentle.

Stagwi'ah said to Hermit Thrush, "Little Brother, are you afraid?"

And Hermit Thrush replied, "Yes, I am."

And the great Eagle asked, "What are you afraid of?"

Hermit Thrush poured out his heart to Stagwi'ah and told him his fears: that he wouldn't be able to fly as high as he should and so wouldn't find his true song.

Stagwi'ah told him, "Hop onto my shoulder, Little Brother. There you will be safe and you'll feel better."

Hermit Thrush thought about this and about the power of Stagwi'ah, the great Eagle. Finally, he hopped onto the Eagle's shoulder and waited for dawn.

When the first rays of dawn touched the Council Rock, the birds all rose as one. The air was filled with the sound of wings. They flew and flew as high as they could, flying as they never had before. Hummingbird flew over the tops of the flowering shrubs and trees, and found a humming song. Robin flew over sunny meadows and saw children playing, and found a cheerful, happy song. Crow flew high above the treetops along the edge of the woods, and found a raucous, playful song.

One by one the birds found their songs and flew slowly back to the Council clearing. By noon, only Stagwi'ah still flew higher and higher, the great wings beating the air, all but invisible to the birds below.

Stagwi'ah flew and flew until he reached the very top of the sky, and gave out a great cry that reached from one edge of the world to the other.

At that cry, Hermit Thrush leaped off the Eagle's shoulder and flew up and up, up and up, and through the hole in the top of the sky that leads to the spirit world.

The Spirits were very taken with this little bird that had travelled so far from its home. They gave to Hermit Thrush a special gift: their own most beautiful song.

Hermit Thrush was filled with joy at the gift and began the flight homeward. Down and down, down and down, until at last the Council Rock could be seen in the clearing, with the other birds gathered all around.

As he neared the clearing, Hermit Thrush found he was still the same shy bird, and avoiding the others, he flew deep into the woods to a private place to reflect on what had befallen a little bird that day.

As dusk fell, Hermit Thrush could no longer keep silent: he opened his throat and began to sing. At the sound, all the forest fell silent, for they knew that such a sweet, achingly beautiful song could only come from the Spirits themselves.[110]

Book of Coming Forth into the Light — *1700s* BCE

God is a Spirit, a hidden spirit, the Spirit of spirits, the Great Spirit of Egypt, the divine Spirit or God-Spirit.

God is hidden. Nobody knows his form, nobody has searched out his likeness. He is hidden to gods and humans. He is a secret, a mystery, to all his creatures.

Nobody knows a name by which to call him. His Name is hidden. His Name is a secret to all his children. His names are without number, his names are many; nobody knows the number thereof.

God is Truth. He lives through Truth, he feeds on Truth. He is the king of Truth, whose Truth makes free the tongue. He rests on Truth, he creates Truth, he sets up Truth over the world.[111]

Jesus — *100s*

Said to his disciples shortly before his death

And I will ask the Father, and he will give you another comforter – an advocate to be with you, beside you, forever.

It is the Spirit of Truth, which the world does not choose to accept because the world has not contemplated it, nor does it know it through experience.

But you know it from experience because it remains close by you – and will be inside you.

I will not send you away, bereaved like orphans: I am coming towards you![112]

PERSPECTIVE

The mystics consistently speak of two types of name or word. There is the ordinary spoken/written kind, which can be pronounced, silently or out loud. And there is what Mira calls "the jewel of the Name," the mysterious Word or Shabd. This ineffable or unperceivable Name, as Soami Ji of Agra refers to it, is the divine power or energy that creates and sustains the universe.

The bhakti mystics tell us that the Name is not a human sound, name or word at all, and for this reason they sometimes call it God's name, the true name, the eternal name, the unpronounceable name, the unspoken recitation, the secret or hidden name, the nameless.

This power is referred to by thousands of names, some of them specific to the culture they come from ("unstruck unending sound" in India, "way" in China, "secret" in Sufism). Other terms for it are more universal – word, name, song, music, voice, spirit, truth – commonly used to speak of this power in mystic writings throughout the world.

The mystics constantly remind us that this spiritual power is within us, accompanies us everywhere, and manifests within as sound and light. The bhakti practice is an inner attuning of body and mind to that power. As Paltu explains, we need to quieten the mind and withdraw our consciousness from the body to the spiritual "cave," the eye centre or focal point deep within, in order to hear the melody that "speaks so sweetly."

Once attuned and at one with the inner sound, the practitioner makes the journey of evolving consciousness – by merging in higher and higher frequencies of this eternal power.

In many cultures the mystics avoid writing even in general terms about the nature of the spiritual practice; such discussions are private, between teacher and disciple. In places where there is freedom of religious expression, the mystics may be more open in their writings. And certain mystics, like Kabir, Dadu and Paltu, speak out boldly regardless.

What we find in the writings of the bhakti mystics, from medieval to modern times, are numerous references to three fundamental aspects of the meditation process: mental repetition, inner contemplation and inner listening.

Simran or *zikr* is a focusing practice involving the silent repetition of sacred names of God, a form of interior or mental prayer. Any kind of inward focus leads to seeing the inner light and hearing the inner sound, but it does not necessarily result in evolution of consciousness. Under the guidance of a true teacher, the regular practice of meditative repetition and contemplation are said to deepen the inward concentration, gradually increasing one's receptivity to the pulling power of the sound and its purifying and strengthening effect on body, mind and soul.

The process of interior listening is referred to by the mystics in this section with various expressions, all of them referring to an inner, not a physical, reality: listening to the bells, hearing the melody or the voice of the Beloved, singing hymns or the song of praise, finding and singing one's true song or song of the Spirits, receiving the comforter or Spirit of Truth, and so on. Whether veiled or open, mystic writings – especially in the Naam bhakti tradition – are full of references to the inner practice of listening and hearing the Sound or Shabd, also known as meditation on the Name.

For many disciples meditation may feel as productive as pushing against a huge rock. The mind is not easily persuaded to focus and turn inwards – and that is the unavoidable first stage on the mystic journey. But the bhakti mystics say that as long as the disciple keeps going with the practice, the lack of results is immaterial: one makes headway by trying. It is even said the disciple makes effort only by the teacher's grace; and when the disciple does make effort, the teacher showers more grace so the disciple continues to make effort.

The reason the disciple makes headway is that although the mind may resist all efforts to focus within, the master cannot resist a disciple's willingness to persist in the face of failure. When the satguru or true teacher so chooses, he makes the disciple worthy, fit to receive Naam: that mysterious gift of realization, the attainment of our true potential – oneness with the infinite.

Yearning

Yearning is the intense pain
of separation from the Beloved.
It consumes the mature practitioner
when disparate thoughts and emotions
are transformed through love,
humility, séva and meditation
into the laserlike focus of longing
for the Beloved,
erasing and replacing
all other impressions on the mind.

1. **Tulsi of Hathras**
   Obsessed with longing for the Beloved p.114
   jin piy ki birha basai
   - Ramon Lull: The lover was all alone
   - David: I rise before dawn
   - Khusro: Dusk wherever I turn

2. **Bahu**
   What your heart desires, it does not get p.117
   jo dil mangé hové naahee~
   - Thérèse de Lisieux: No other compass
   - Tohfah of Syria: Don't be amazed
   - Kabir and the king of Bukhara ~ A story

3. **Dadu**
   It's cruel p.121
   ajahu~ na nikasai praaN kaThor
   - Jesus: A woman giving birth
   - The Mother: A new birth
   - Ansari: The ultimate need

4. **Mira**
Dear Wanderer, all day I watch for you p.124
jogiya ji nisadin jo'oo~ baaT
   - Alfred Tennyson: In Memoriam
   - Isaiah: You shall weep no more!

5. **Ramdas**
My heart is burning up p.127
har/i darsan ka'u méra man/u bahu taptai
   - Ancient Egyptian: Thirst in the desert
   - Laurent de la résurrection: Knock, persevere in knocking
   - William Law: Hunger

6. **Bullah**
It would be nice if you came sometime p.129
kadi aa mil biraho~ sataa'i noo~
   - Shams: I am that bird who is hanging by both feet
   - Eckhart: God's need

Perspective p.131

Tulsi of Hathras

1700s–1843

When you are obsessed with longing
 for the Beloved
Your body becomes weaker and weaker.
Tears flow far, seeking him.
Body and mind ache – for him.

The stream of my love has overflowed
In these monsoon months when lovers reunite.
Day and night I long for him.
Rain pours.

This pain for the Beloved, it's consumed me.
My attention can go nowhere else.
I'm a moonbird with my moon –
My eyes want only him.

Thundering clouds burst with lightning.
Dazzling flashes tantalize peacocks and rainbirds:
"Beloved, Beloved!" – persistent cry.
I'm drained. Restless. Nothing left of body.

I listen to the Sound
But patience, tranquillity, doesn't come.
Why don't I write a letter – send it to the Beloved!
I'll make mind and soul my messengers –
They can go where I cannot,
To his home beyond going.

If I were to hear from my Beloved –
A hint, a word that he's coming –
My heart would break with joy!
Day and night I long for him.
Rain pours.

Tulsi, when you are possessed
With yearning for the Beloved,
Nothing is left to tie you to the world –
It's just a speck![113]

Ramon Lull *1233–1315*

The lover was alone, in the shade of a great tree.

People passed by that place and asked him why he was all alone, and the lover replied:

"I am alone now that I have seen and heard you; before, I was in the company of my Beloved!"

The Beloved reveals himself to the lover, clothed in new and scarlet robes. He stretches out his arms to embrace him, he inclines his head to kiss him – and he remains on high that he might ever seek him.[114]

David *1040–940* BCE

I rise before dawn and I cry out –
My hope is in your Word!
My eyes open before the watches of the night
That I might meditate on your Word.[115]

Khusro *1253–1325*

Response when first taken to the tomb of his master

The beautiful young woman
Is asleep on her bed of union,
Her face covered by the curtain of her hair.
Come, Khusro, let us go home now –
Dusk has settled wherever I turn.[116]

Bahu

1628–1691

What your heart desires,
It does not get –
Fulfilment always out of reach. *Lord...*

The Friend doesn't give you the remedy
For your heart, nor does love tug the reins
And turn back. *Beloved...*

That's why in the arena of love
You find nothing but fire –
Fierce, blazing fire. *Lord...*

Bahu, I give my life for anyone
Who manages to keep going ahead,
One step at a time. *Beloved...*[117]

Thérèse de Lisieux

1873–1897

Now abandonment alone guides me – I have no other compass![118]

Tohfah of Syria *800s*

Don't be amazed at those murder'd
In the dust of the Friend's door:
Be amazed at how anyone can survive
With soul intact![119]

Kabir and the king of Bukhara ~ A story *1400s*

Seekers are drawn to a mystic like moths to a flame, regardless of geographical distance. So it was that Ibrahim Adham, the king of Bukhara, left his kingdom in search of a teacher who could give him enlightenment. He somehow found his way from his home in Uzbekistan in the far north, southeast across today's Afghanistan, Pakistan and India – searching and inquiring for spiritual teachers all the way, never satisfied until he came at last to the satsang of Kabir in the city of Varanasi.

But when the king asked Kabir for initiation, Kabir declined, saying: "There is nothing in common between a king and a poor weaver like myself. How can two such people get on together?" The king begged Kabir to grant him Naam, saying he had not come as a king but as a beggar and was asking only for spirituality and Kabir's blessings. Lo'i, Kabir's wife, was touched and asked Kabir to accept him. Kabir let him stay.

And so the king lived in the simple compound of Kabir's house, sleeping on the ground, helping with the women's jobs of a weaver's family – preparing the warp of the men's looms with strong thread, learning from the women how to spin yarn from coarse wool, carrying water from the well in a large clay pot on his head, sweeping, washing clothes, and anything else he was asked to do.

This went on for six years until one day Lo'i pointed out to Kabir how long the king had served them and how uncomplaining he had been. "Isn't it time to give him something?" Kabir shook his head. "His heart is not yet clean." Lo'i said, "Dear husband, I find that hard to believe! Here he is, a king, and we are poor weavers: he has eaten our dry bread and served us all this time, never refusing to do anything we tell him to. How can his heart not be pure?"

"All right," said Kabir, "do this: gather up the sweepings from the house, take it up to the roof terrace and wait. As the king passes below, let it fall on his head. Hide yourself and listen to what he says. Then come and tell me."

Lo'i did as Kabir said. The king came walking back to the house from an errand and as he approached the door, he was dowsed in a shower of dust from above. Angrily he called out, "What a pity – if it were Bukhara, you'd pay dearly for this!"

Lo'i told Kabir what the king had said. "It's as I told you – his heart is not yet pure: it's not worthy of receiving the gift of Naam."

And so another six years passed, with the king working just as hard as he had in the first six years. Finally one day Kabir said to Lo'i, "The vessel is ready." Surprised, she said, "But I don't see any difference now from how he was before. He has continued to be uncomplaining and hard-working, even when we have only a couple of chickpeas left to eat."

Kabir said: "You want to see the difference? Remember last time you gathered up the sweepings and took it onto the roof terrace? Well, this time go outside into the lane and collect the smelliest filth you can find. Take a full load of it up to the terrace and let it fall on the king, just as you did the first time."

The next day at an opportune moment, Lo'i dropped the load of refuse on the king's head. The king burst out laughing. Dripping with filth, he touched his forehead in a gesture of acceptance, and then looked up and said: "Well done, whoever you are! My mind was full of ego. This is just the treatment it needed! Thank you."

When Lo'i reported the king's response, Kabir smiled. "As I told you, there is nothing wanting but Naam."

A little later he called the king to him. As Kabir gazed into the king's eyes, his soul immediately ascended, consciousness merging from Shabd to Shabd as he traversed the inner realms and ultimately merged in the Source.

When it's a sant satguru like Kabir and a disciple like the king of Bukhara, what else would you expect! Getting the fruit of Naam is no small thing: the purer your heart, the quicker Naam takes effect.

When the king came back to himself, Kabir said: "Now you can go sit wherever you wish. Your devotion is complete."

Ibrahim Adham returned to Bukhara, but not as king. His sons went on ruling in his place, while he spent the rest of his life as an unknown, earning his bread through odd jobs here and there, and keeping most of his time for solitude – to enjoy the gift of Kabir.[120]

Dadu

1544–1603

It's cruel –
Why am I still breathing?
So many days have passed without seeing you,
My beautiful Beloved –
So many days.

Night moves at the speed of an aeon,
Each second dragging through the dark
Till dawn.
You promised to come
But you haven't till yet.
What's keeping you away,
Thief of my heart?

I've been gazing down your path –
My eyes see no sign that you're coming.
I'm a moonbird without the moon –
Restless, anguished,
Separated from you.[121]

Jesus *100s*

A woman giving birth to a child has pain because her time has come; but when the little one is born she forgets the anguish, she is so filled with joy and grace that she has brought a child into the world.

So with you: now indeed you are depressed with grief, but I shall see you within and your heart will rejoice – and no one shall take away that grace-filled joy of yours![122]

The Mother *1878–1973*

The change of consciousness and its preparation have often been compared with the formation of the chicken in the egg: till the very last second the egg remains the same, there is no change, and it is only when the chicken is completely formed, absolutely alive, that with its little beak it makes by itself a hole in the shell and comes out.

Something similar takes place at the moment of the change of consciousness. For a long time you have the impression that nothing is happening, that your consciousness is the same as usual – and if you have an intense aspiration, you even feel a resistance, as though you were knocking against a wall that does not yield. But when you are ready within, a last effort – the pecking in the shell of the being – and everything opens and you are projected into another consciousness.

This may happen suddenly, spontaneously, quite unexpectedly. I don't think one can go through to the other side gradually. There is rather a kind of accumulation of power inside, an intensification of the need and an endurance in the effort, which becomes free from all fear, all anxiety, all calculation: a need so imperative one no longer cares about the consequences.

One is like an explosive that nothing can resist, and one bursts out from one's prison in a blaze of light.

After that one can no longer fall back again.

It is truly a new birth.[123]

Ansari *1006–1088*

O Lord, I am a beggar, yet I am asking of you more than a thousand kings might ask, each with something he needs from you alone. I have come to ask you to give me yourself.[124]

Mira

1498–1573

Dear Wanderer, all day I watch for you.
All night, too, my eyes on the road.
My feet can't walk this path –
It's too difficult, too narrow and steep.
How can I reach that inaccessible place
Where the journey begins?

Once he came to my town, this Wanderer.
He enjoyed himself
But he found no love in my heart.
What a fool I was – so naive, so ignorant:
Why didn't I keep him here,
Entice him, persuade him to stay?
Why did I let him go!

I've been waiting ever since –
Waiting, watching for my Wanderer.
No sign of him yet.
Oh Wanderer, come inside,
Put out this wildfire of longing –
It's burning me up, my body's on fire.

Maybe my Wanderer is no longer alive.
Either that or he's forgotten me.
What can I do?
Friends, where can I go?
I've cried for him so much
My eyes have gone blind.

Wanderer,
I'm in so much pain inside
Because of you.
Won't you come –
I belong to you!

Mira is confused –
Agonized by separation.
Now life leaks out in painful breaths –
Without you.[125]

Alfred Tennyson *1809–1892*

But what am I?
An infant crying in the night:
An infant crying for the light:
And with no language but a cry.[126]

Isaiah *700s BCE*

You shall weep no more!

He will be very gracious to you at the voice of your cry: the moment he hears it, he will answer you.

And though the Lord gives you the bread of adversity and the water of affliction, yet your teacher shall not withdraw himself any more, but your eyes shall see your teacher.

And your ears shall hear a word behind you, saying: This is the way, walk in it – when you turn to the right hand and when you turn to the left.[127]

Ramdas

1534–1581

My heart is burning up
For a sight of God –
Like a thirsty person without water.
The arrow of God's love
Has pierced through my mind.
Only the Lord God knows my agony,
The pain deep inside.

Anybody who speaks to me
About my divine Beloved
Is my brother, my friend!
Come and join me, sisters,
Let us recite the qualities of my Lord
And take to the satguru's path
Of patience.

My heart is burning up
For a sight of God –
Like a thirsty person without water.
Oh God, fulfil your servant Nanak's desire:
Your darshan, a body at peace![128]

Ancient Egyptian *1200s BCE*

Thou sweet well, for those who thirst in the desert! It is closed to those who speak, but open to those who are silent. When the silent ones come, lo, they find the well.[129]

Laurent de la résurrection *1614–1691*

Written shortly before his death
Knock, persevere in knocking, and I answer for it that he will open to you in his due time and grant you all at once what he has deferred during many years.

I am always happy. All the world suffers, and I, who deserve the severest discipline, feel joys so continual and so great that I can scarce contain them.[130]

William Law *1686–1761*

The hunger of the soul is the first necessity. All else will follow.[131]

Bullah

1680–1758

It would be nice if you came sometime
To visit this beloved of yours,
Agonizing here in separation from you.

If you were in love, you'd groan and cry.
What do you know of the pain you inflict on others?
It would be nice if you came to visit sometime.

If somebody is interested in buying love, tell them
First give you their head as down-payment.
Oh, please come visit this beloved of yours!

Those dutiful meditators have all passed me by.
What about me – will you let the world laugh?
I'm just agonizing here, separated from you.

Carried away by a flood of grief on waves of tyranny –
You've stranded me on a sandbank, midstream.
Any chance you might come?

I abandoned my parents, forgot my friends,
Sacrificed myself for you – for God's sake, come:
I cannot bear this separation any more.[132]

Shams *1184–1247*

I am that bird who is hanging by both feet. Yes, I hang, but in the snare of the Beloved I hang, and suddenly I say, "Hello, how are you?" – for I was seeking this captivity!

I was not seeking the storehouse; I wanted the mines of silver and gold. I was rather avoiding this place and its treasure because nothing suited me but him.

If a flower does not suit you,
Then its thorn will;
If the pulpit does not suit you,
Then the gallows will. *Anon.*

You laid claim to my heart;
I sacrificed my life also.
Is there something more to do?
Are we still indebted to you? *Rumi*[133]

Eckhart *1250s–1329*

God can no more do without us than we can do without him.[134]

PERSPECTIVE

The mystics say that *bireh*, the intense pain of yearning one may experience in separation from the Beloved, is not an emotion – nor is it a state one can cultivate or stimulate. What most of us experience is a variety of emotions, devotional and otherwise, that last for a while. Spiritual yearning, on the other hand, is permanent, incessant and inconceivably intense.

It is said that yearning is a state of consciousness only a spiritually mature person can handle. It takes tremendous inner strength and unwavering faith and devotion to stand the all-consuming love-pain of separation, which literally eradicates the self, allowing no thought of anything but the Beloved to enter the mind.

Tulsi of Hathras, Dadu, Mira, Ramdas, Bullah – all the mystics hint at the indescribable pain of separation. In their songpoems they use words like restless, anguished, agonized, burning, but few of us grasp the intensity of that state: unending consumption in the fires of love. Bahu says, with the empathy of somebody who personally knows it: I give my life for anyone who manages to keep going ahead, one step at a time.

Most of us could not tolerate or internalize the kind of obsession described in the songpoems on yearning. But when the teacher knows a disciple is capable of digesting and containing the intensity of the love, the longing and the strange joy of being obsessed with the Beloved, then he gives the special grace of yearning.

Why grace? Because, as Tulsi of Hathras explains, deep yearning in separation frees the disciple from whatever keeps their attention tied down to the world. It purifies the heart for receiving the supreme energy of Spirit and makes the lover completely one-pointed – the intensity of the longing caused by the pulling of the Beloved.

This extraordinary attracting process impels the consciousness inward, onward – the progress in relation to the intensity of the fire, which obliterates everything within the disciple except longing. Moth to a flame – the person consumed by the agony of separation is ceaselessly circling and spiralling towards the source, inwardly burning to be one, to lose the self entirely in the eternal hidden Presence: to become the Beloved.

Perhaps the most mysterious aspect of the agonizing fire of separation is that no mystic is willing to give it up. Some of them explain there is as much pleasure in yearning as there is in being in the presence of the Beloved.

In an entirely pragmatic manner, the bhakti teachers advise their disciples to keep inner yearning as the goal and to work towards it systematically with meditation and séva (service). The pain of longing is the legacy of devotion, given when the disciple is mature enough to handle it. Meanwhile, like a child being assigned small jobs in the family business until she is old enough to take on other responsibilities, disciples are told to keep going with the daily practice as preparation for that day to come.

Love

Love is the gift of the master:
the non-physical merging
of one being in another being –
of consciousness, lover,
in the inner Presence, Beloved.

1. **Farid**
Farid, the rain has churned the lanes to mud p.136
fareedaa~ galee'é chikkaR/u door ghar/u
- Shams: The meeting of two friends
- Nizamuddin and Khusro ~ A story
- Aurobindo: The nature of devotion

2. **Kabir**
Kabir, the cloud of love came by p.140
kabeer baadal prém ko
- Chuang-tse: A disciple complained
- *Joseph and Aseneth:* By the beckoning of his eyes
- Mechthild von Magdeburg: Fused in one

3. **Ravidas**
The bonds of love p.143
ja'u ham baandhé moh phaas
- Jana and Namdev ~ A story
- John: To know God
- 13th-century German: The pathless way

4. **Paltu**
Mind has gone mad with love for the Friend p.147
prém divaana man yaar

- Unknown psalmist: Anguished longing
- Rumi: The moon has fallen in love
- Nanak and Lehna ~ A story

5. **Dadu**
Until you offer your head p.150
jab lag sees na saumpiyé

- Jesus: The pure in heart
- Thérèse de Lisieux: Love calls to love
- Ayaaz and the pearl ~ A story

6. **Gobind Singh**
I'm telling the truth p.153
saach kahoo~ sun lého sabhee

- Juan de la Cruz: Hunting the Beloved
- Julian of Norwich: Give me yourself

Perspective p.155

Farid

1173–1265

Farid, the rain has churned the lanes to mud.
The house of the one I love is far away.
If I go my shawl will get soaked –
If I stay, the bond of love will break.

Let my shawl get soaking wet!
God, make the rain pour down!
I must go meet that beloved friend
Or the bond of love will break.[135]

Shams

1184–1247

The only purpose of the world's existence is the meeting of two friends who face God and turn away from worldly desire.

The sun, *Shams,* illuminates the whole world. Molana Rumi sees that light shine from my mouth, from my speech; it glows even beneath black words.

This *Shams* has its back to anyone else, but faces the skies above and illuminates all, above and below.

Shams is facing Molana because Molana is facing Shams.[136]

Nizamuddin and Khusro ~ A story *1200s*

Nizamuddin was a mystic who lived in thirteenth-century Delhi. Once, a poor man with a daughter to marry came to him and begged for his help. What do mystics have to give! Even his langar, the free kitchen, was barely able to keep going. Nizamuddin told the man: "Stay for three days. Whatever offerings come during that time, you can take."

Will of the Lord! Nothing came on the first day, nothing on the second, nothing on the third. The poor man came to say goodbye to Nizamuddin, and mumbled, "I'm leaving now, sir. My luck is out." Nizamuddin said, "You're leaving? All right, you take my sandals. They are the only thing I possess. Sell them and you will get enough to buy at least one day's supply of food." The poor man thanked Nizamuddin, accepted the shoes and set out for his village, despairing that he would ever be able to marry off his daughter.

As he trudged along the dirty dusty road, he saw approaching him a large caravan of richly appointed, heavily laden camels. It was Ameer Khusro, poet, musician, historian of princes and kings, returning from Kabul after retiring from the ruler's service.

Khusro himself was riding at the head of the caravan. Suddenly he noticed the fragrance of his beloved master, right when he came near a poor man walking along at the side of the road. Just as Khusro was wondering to himself "Where is my Beloved's fragrance coming from?", he rode past the poor man and now felt the fragrance coming from behind. Puzzled and surprised, Khusro stopped at once and got down from his camel. He called out to the traveller, "Who are you, brother? Where are you coming from?"

The poor man explained that he'd gone to Delhi in the hope of getting some money from Nizamuddin Auliya to pay for the wedding of his daughter. "But faqeers go barefoot and they're as poor as they come. Anyway, when God doesn't give, the saints don't either."

Khusro loved his master and his heart was pierced by the man's words. "Did he give you anything?" The poor man held up Nizamuddin's sandals: "He gave me these!"

Khusro said, "Do you want to sell them? I can give you whatever price you name." "You're welcome to them. I was going to sell them in the next village to buy something to eat because I'm hungry."

What did Khusro do? He kept the two camels he and his family were riding and one more for luggage. All the rest – with their rich loads and his retinue of servants – he gave to the poor man: "Now go and get your daughter married!"

Thanking him again and again, the poor man went off with the caravan, unable to believe his good fortune – all from an old pair of shoes!

Shortly after the encounter on the road, Khusro reached the home of his master. He carefully dusted off the sandals and then went to the master and placed them at his feet.

"And what did you give for such an old pair of shoes?" said Nizamuddin. Khusro bowed: "Sir, whatever I had, I gave it all." Nizamuddin smiled. "You got them cheap!"

Later, commenting on the depth of Khusro's love, Nizamuddin went so far as to say: "Don't let Khusro come anywhere near my tomb or he'll break it wide open to reach me!"

This state belongs only to lovers. As Kabir says:

> If you give your head
> In the hope of finding a master,
> Look on it as a bargain![137]

Aurobindo *1872–1950*

The nature of bhakti is adoration, worship, self-offering to what is greater than oneself.

Bhakti is not an experience, it is a state of the heart and soul.

The deeper the emotion and the more intense the bhakti, the greater is the force for realization and transformation.

It is oftenest through intensity of emotion that the psychic being awakes and there is an opening of the inner doors to the divine.[138]

Kabir

1398–1518

Kabir, the cloud of love came by
And the rain poured down on me –
Soul got soaked, and every plant in sight
Has turned a brilliant green!

When I was, the master was not;
Now the master is, I am not.
The lane of love is so narrow, Kabir,
There's not room for two.

There's nothing of mine
In me; whatever there is
Is yours. In returning yours to you,
Says Kabir, what credit to me!

Twenty-four hours, every moment,
I stay alive by gazing at you.
Why should I close my eyes? says Kabir –
In everybody it's the Beloved I see.[139]

Chuang-tse *400s* BCE

A disciple complained to Keng San Chu, disciple of Lao Tzu: "The other disciples get your meaning and put it in practice; I cannot. You tell me: 'Hold your being secure and quiet, keep your life collected in its own centre. Do not allow your thoughts to be disturbed.' But however hard I try, Tao is only a word in my ear. It does not ring any bells inside."

Keng San replied: "I have nothing more to say. Bantams do not hatch goose eggs. Why not go south and see Lao Tzu?"

The disciple got some supplies, travelled seven days and seven nights, alone, and came to Lao Tzu.

After many days of effort and confusion, the disciple groaned: "I am like a sick man who takes medicine that makes him ten times worse. Just tell me the first elements. I will be satisfied!"

Lao Tzu replied: "You want the first elements? The infant has them. Free from care, unaware of self, he acts without reflection, stays where he is put, does not know why, does not figure things out, just goes along with them, is part of the current. These are the first elements!"

The disciple asked: "Is this perfection?"

Lao replied: "Not at all. It is only the beginning. This melts the ice.

"This enables you to unlearn – so you can be led by Tao, be a child of Tao.

"If you persist in trying to attain what is never attained (it is Tao's gift!), if you persist in making effort to obtain what effort cannot get, if you persist in reasoning about what cannot be understood, you will be destroyed by the very thing you seek.

"To know when to stop, to know when you can get no further by your own action – this is the right beginning!"[140]

Joseph and Aseneth ~ A story *200s*

Then Joseph stretched out his arms and by the beckoning of his eyes called Aseneth. And Aseneth also stretched out her arms and ran to Joseph, and fell on his neck and embraced him, and they entered into the life of the Spirit and were united to one another.

And Joseph kissed Aseneth and gave her the Spirit of Life; then he kissed her a second time and gave her the Spirit of Wisdom; then he kissed her a third time and gave her the Spirit of Truth.

And when they had embraced one another for a long time, intertwining their hands like chains, Aseneth said to Joseph, "Come with me, my Lord, and enter our house."[141]

Mechthild von Magdeburg *1207–1294*

I am in thee and thou in Me; we could not be closer, for we two are fused in one, poured into one mould. Thus unwearied shall we remain forever.[142]

Ravidas

1414–1540

If you have caught me in the snares of attachment,
I have tied you with the bonds of love!
You can try all you want to get free –
I freed myself by adoring you.
Beloved, you know exactly how it is with me,
So how can you stand to act this way?

You have caught me like a fish,
Sliced me open, cut me up, marinated me,
Cooked me well – and now
You're making a meal of it,
Chewing me bit by bit. Even then,
Fish never forget water...
Beloved, you know exactly how it is with me!

Nobody can just claim God as their father:
It's love that conquers the King!
There's an inflammation,
A film of attachment,
That has permeated everybody's eyes –
The only ones not afflicted are devotees.

Says Ravidas, All my devotion,
Welling up inside, is bound up in just one.
Who can understand what I mean!
The reason I adore you hasn't changed:
I'm bearing the pain of it even now.
Beloved, you know exactly how it is with me –
How can you stand to act this way![143]

Jana and Namdev ~ A story *1300s*

Jana, poet and childlike devotee of the mystic Namdev, serves in Namdev's family most of her life, from the time she is orphaned as a child. She looks after Namdev from his birth and throughout his childhood, and then later becomes his disciple and is responsible for preparing the family's food.

One day Jana sees the Lord himself eating lunch with Namdev and his family. Agonized, she sits outside by the cooking pots, quietly crying her eyes out, upset with Namdev for not inviting her to join the others.

One of her songpoems recalls her turmoil: "Your wife and mother stay at your feet, your sons are placed proudly in front, but this woman is kept on the doorstep – no room for the lowly inside. O God, how I want your embrace! When will you call the slave Jani your own?"

From inside the family's hut, Namdev immediately feels her pain and stops eating. Excusing himself, he says, "The food is very nice, but I find I'm not hungry." He leaves his family to finish their meal and takes his half-eaten food outside, putting the plate gently into Jana's hands. "Janatai, this is for you."

Overcome by her own tears and his kindness, Jana gratefully accepts the gift of his food – *prasaad*, a blessing from her satguru. Unable to eat any of it right then, she takes the plate to her sleeping place and keeps it there, covered with a cloth.

That night, the story goes that the Lord himself comes to Jana in her hut. He says, "I was eating with Nama but as I had not invited you, the food gave me no pleasure. Now I am hungry – please give me something to eat."

Babbling in her joy, Jana says, "O Sadguru, dear Master, what shall I give you to eat? Lord knows, I'm your slave, a powerless servant of Nama. It's not proper to give you what is left over: you are the Lord of the universe! How can I give you dry bread? Don't put me to the test, my lifetime companion, my friend! And bear in mind, my Lord, it is long past midnight!"

Godlike, the radiant Beloved replies: "Everything that is given to anyone is mine to begin with. So where is that food? Feed me, my child!"[144]

John 100s

One who does not love has not realized God, for God is love.[145]

Be as a child – be deaf, be blind! Your own self must cease to be. Put aside all I-ness: discard it, all this nothingness!

Leave behind place and time and images – follow the narrow pathless way. Like this you will discover clues to the desert.

O soul of mine, through God go in: sink your I into the Nothingness of God – sink into the immeasurable flood!

If I flee from you, you come to me;
If I leave my self, it is you I find,
O essential goodness![146]

Paltu

1700s–1800s

Mind has gone mad with love for the Friend.
I'm his – the guru can do what he wants with me.
Day and night, waves pour through me
From deep inside.
Who can remember to eat or drink!

In the cave of Trikuti's sky
There's an alleyway in a garden of flowers.
Right there I found him.
We merged, inside.

A lotus with a thousand petals
In a mountain lake:
That's where the bumblebee was caught,
Enticed inside.

The slave Paltu,
He's an addict but takes no drugs –
A madman intoxicated night and day:
A garden, a lotus, a lake… Mad
With love for the Friend![147]

Unknown psalmist *500s BCE*

Anguish for your house has eaten me up.[148]

Rumi *1207–1273*

Do not leave me: hide in my heart like a secret, wind around my head like a turban. "I come and go as I please," you say, "swift as a heartbeat." You can tease me as much as you like, but never leave me.

Last night in a gathering I caught a glimpse of my Beloved. Too embarrassed to embrace him, I put my face against his cheek, pretending to whisper something in his ear.

Do you know, knower, what the night is? It is the sanctuary of lovers. On this glorious night I am drunk with the moon. The moon has fallen in love and the night has gone mad.[149]

Nanak and Lehna ~ A story *1500s*

Lehna was a devoted disciple of Nanak and lived in Kartarpur in Nanak's house – as a sévadar, serving the master.

Nanak's wife and sons became jealous as they saw, day after day, the love of Nanak for his devotee and the intense devotion of Lehna for his master. Eventually, the family insisted that Lehna should be turned out.

Nanak called Lehna and explained the situation to him. He said, "You'll have to go."

"Yes, sir, I'll go," Lehna said. "But I cannot live without you."

Nanak replied: "And I cannot live without you." So Lehna stayed.

He stayed and was renamed Angad, 'limb of my limbs'. Nanak said: "Lehna" (similar to *laiNa*, meaning 'to take') "has taken all I have. Now he has become Angad, one with my essence."

In time, when Guru Nanak left this world, he made Angad his spiritual successor. Thereafter, each successor signed his writings 'Nanak' – the only identity they were aware of.

Guru Arjan, the fifth teacher in the line of Nanak, compiled a spiritual anthology in 1604 known as the Adi Granth. He differentiated the five Nanaks in the anthology by referring to them as M1, M2, M3, M4, M5 – *mahila* ('woman, wife') number 1, 2, 3, 4, 5 – consorts, every one, of the Beloved.[150]

Dadu

1544–1603

Until you offer your head
You'll not experience love.
The lover who is not afraid to die, Dadu,
Is the one who drinks the cup.

The lover has drunk the cup of light
In the skies within.
Twenty-four hours it's only the face of God,
Says Dadu, that keeps him alive.

Whatever you've given me,
Take all of it back –
Without you my mind knows no peace.
Just give me darshan! says Dadu.

The lover has become the Beloved –
That is called love.
Dadu, God himself becomes the lover
Of such a beloved.[151]

Jesus *100s*

Blessed are the pure in heart, for they shall see God.[152]

Thérèse de Lisieux *1873–1897*

Love calls to love, and mine longs to fill the abyss of yours in its flight to you, but it is not even a drop of dew lost in that Sea. If I am to love you as you love me, I must borrow your love; I can find peace no other way.[153]

Ayaaz and the pearl ~ A story *1100s*

Tales about the loyalty and devotion of the slave Ayaaz for his master, the king of Ghazni, have been told for centuries by Sufis to illustrate qualities needed on the inner path. This story of Ayaaz and the pearl is based on the Persian tale told by the mystic Shams of Tabriz, back in the 1200s.

One day King Mahmood decided to test his advisers to find out whether any of them were truly wise. So he took a precious pearl, an extraordinary gem, handed it to his minister and told him to break it.

"How can I break this pearl? One-fourth of it is worth the entire kingdom!" said the minister. "You are right," said the king and kissed his eyes, showing approval and reassurance.

Then the king handed the pearl to his chamberlain. "Is it not good?" said the king. "A hundred thousand times good," answered the chamberlain. "Now break it!" said the king. "Sire, how can I break it when it is so valuable?" And the king answered, "Excellent!"

The pearl went from hand to hand until just one person remained: the king's slave, his beloved Ayaaz. The king thought to himself, "My Ayaaz!" He was shivering with worry and concern lest Ayaaz, too, behave like the others. Then he held out the pearl and said, "O slave, take it – and break it."

Ayaaz pulled two stones from his pocket and broke the pearl with one stroke. It shattered like dust. "Ahh!" shouted everyone. "What are the Ahhs and the shouting?" Ayaaz asked. "Why did you break such a precious pearl?" they said.

Ayaaz said quietly: "Is not the king's order far more precious than this jewel?" Everybody lowered their heads, sighing from their hearts a hundred thousand times, thinking "What have we done?"

The king ordered his executioners to clear the room, but Ayaaz said, "O forbearing king, forgiveness is worthier." The king acquiesced and then quoted a line of Arabic verse:

> I have given all of myself to you:
> I am preoccupied only with you![154]

Gobind Singh

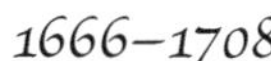

1666–1708

I'm telling the truth –
Hear it, all of you:
Only those who love
Get the Lord.[155]

Juan de la Cruz

1542–1591

Bent on a venture of love, and not for lack of hope, I flew high, so high, it brought my quarry within reach…

In order to succeed in this sacred enterprise, I had to fly so high that I lost sight of my self. In spite of all this, the extreme of my flight was not enough: but love went higher yet and so brought my quarry within reach.

When I went higher up I was dazzled, and the hardest of my victories was won in the dark: because the venture was for love, I leapt blind, pitch darkness, and went high, so high, it brought my quarry within reach.

The higher I went on this quest, so intense, the more I found I was depressed, exhausted, brought low. I said: Nobody can reach it – which discouraged me so much I went higher and higher, bringing my quarry within reach.

In the strangest of ways I flew a thousand flights in one: when hope is for heaven, your hoping is equal to your quest. I hoped only for this chance – and didn't lack for hope! Somehow I went high, so high, it brought my quarry within reach.

Bent on a venture of love, and not for lack of hope, I flew high, so high, it brought my quarry within reach...[156]

Julian of Norwich *1342–1416*

God, of your goodness give me yourself, for you are enough for me and I can ask for nothing that is less which can pay you full worship. And if I ask anything less, always I am in want; only in you do I have everything.[157]

PERSPECTIVE

The mystics say there is no chronology in love – that first one feels love and then one feels longing, or the reverse. We cannot feel longing without love, and we cannot love without longing. And who knows when the seed of love and longing was first planted!

The mystics encourage us that we are all born with a drop of love, and are only alive because we have love within us. They say we would not be drawn to a spiritual teacher if we did not have love. Once initiated and meditating, what we want now is more and more love – a desire that is the natural outcome of the meditation process.

The selections in the Love section are a series of portraits depicting the lover/devotee in relation to the Beloved. They give a picture of what unconditional love looks like – this merging of two in the oneness of Spirit or Shabd. Paltu calls it the "madness" of the blissful love state beyond the mind; Ravidas talks of disciple and Beloved being inextricably tied to one another by bonds of love that liberate the disciple from all bonds of attachment to the world.

The portraits also convey something of the intensity inherent in this merging process. For the drop to become one with the ocean of Being, the small self must dissolve; in union, says Kabir, there is no room for two. Ravidas says the individual mind is gradually "chewed" by the Beloved until nothing of self remains: There's nothing of mine in me, affirms Kabir.

Once surrendered to the Beloved, awareness is focused on love longing – the thirst of fish for water, says Ravidas: a thirst that never leaves, that turns the disciple into what Paltu calls an "addict" who takes no drugs but remains totally intoxicated night and day – on love for the Friend, the Beloved.

For disciples like that, love means responding to the call, the inner pull. Facing constantly in the direction of the Beloved, wherever they may be, they feel what Shams calls the hidden sun of the Beloved's presence and they breathe his fragrance, as Khusro did. In that alert wakefulness, such lovers live focused on love and longing for the hidden Presence, satisfied only with what the mystics call *darshan* – the bliss and complete absorption of beholding the Beloved, inside or outside.

Is it an easy process to establish such a love relationship? The mystics make it clear that becoming a lover will require everything we have; that as long as we hold back anything, we will not experience the truth Gobind Singh refers to: Only those who love get the Lord.

But when the lover is brought to surrender all for love of the Beloved – ego, mind, self, desire, thought, all trace of "I" – then the unimaginable takes place: the Ocean falls in love and merges in the drop!

Union

Union is the eternal
ever-present spiritual reality;
realization of it is the goal of life –
the awakening of consciousness, here and now,
merged in the ocean of divine energy,
the source.
The mystics' love poetry –
a reflection of the inexpressible:
ecstasy, and oneness with the divine.

1. **Paltu**
An ascetic was wandering through the town p.160
phirai ik jogi nagar bhulaana
- Bayazid Bastami: Lost in God
- Liu I-ming: Merging with the Tao
- The rising of the sun ~ A story
- Namdev: When I see him

2. **Soami Ji of Agra**
What a night! p.165
mangal mool aaj ki rajni
- *Odes of Solomon:* Come, all you who thirst
- Juan de la Cruz: On a night of darkness
- Isaac Luria: Impossible to express

3. **Kabir**
After such a long time p.169
bahut dinan thai~ mai~ preetam paayé
- Moses Maimonides: Overflowing with love
- Jana: Just God
- Shams: Did you sleep in the morning
- Rumi: I drank from his flaming cup

4. **Mira**
It's raining – make it pour! p.172
méha barsavo karé ré

- Sarmad: My heart searched for your fragrance
- Mechthild von Magdeburg:
  Bringing together two lovers

5. **Kabir**
Listen, dear friend p.174
sunu sakhi pee'a mahi jee'u basai

- Catarina of Genoa: My "me"
- *Téra… téra… téra…* ~ A story
- Khusro: One

6. **Bahu**
A lover lost his heart to the Beloved p.176
aashiq shahu dé dil khaRaa'ia

- Gopi Chand's challenge ~ A story
- Chuang-tse: Words forgotten

Perspective p.180

Paltu

1700s–1800s

An ascetic was wandering through the town,
Lost in himself, carefree.
He was rising up within, going from palace to palace,
Mad with ecstasy.
He didn't eat, didn't drink, didn't beg.
He didn't speak, didn't stumble.
But how he danced!
Danced without dancing to a melody no one played.

He found nectar dripping everywhere
In the house of happiness –
Drank from a curving tube.
Whenever you see him, he's full to the brim with love,
Repeating the unrepeatable Name that has no rosary.

This wandering ascetic sounded a horn
In the cave of Trikuti's sky.
He stayed awake in the realm of wakefulness,
Sat in meditation at the confluence of three rivers,
A lover in love with the Lord beyond Lords.

He took a vow of silence when he sat in the Void
But played the music of the unending drum.
By the time he entered the realm of Turiya
He could hardly speak for tears of joy.
And then he began to sing a song,
His voice reverberating – loud, long.

Our jogi became the Sound:
Merged, one Shabd to another.
The granite gates in the skies of Trikuti
Crumbled to dust!

Says the slave Paltu,
Who can separate them now?
The Ocean has merged
In the drop![158]

Bayazid Bastami *804–874*

Bayazid said, "The first time I went into the Holy House I saw the Holy House. The second time, I saw the Lord of the House. The third, I saw neither the House nor its Lord."

Bayazid meant by this, 'I became lost in God, so I knew nothing. If I had seen anything at all, I would have been God.'

An anecdote bears out this interpretation: A man came to the door of Bayazid and called out.

"Who are you looking for?" Bayazid asked.

"Bayazid," the man replied.

"You poor fool!" Bayazid said. "I have been looking for Bayazid for thirty years and cannot find any trace or sign of him."[159]

Liu I-ming *1734–1836*

When wood is exposed for a long time it rots, but if it is fired into charcoal it will never rot. Water and earth combine to make clay, which dissolves in the rain; fire it into brick, however, and it will last indefinitely.

What I realize as I observe this is the Tao of firing to create reality. The reason people are unable to attain the Tao is that they have not yet been fired in the furnace of creation.

If one walks with every step on the ground of reality in the furnace of creation, experiencing everything that comes along, being in the doorway of life and death without wavering, like gold that becomes brighter the more it is fired, like a mirror that becomes clearer the more it is polished, fired and polished to a state of round brightness, clean nakedness, bare freedom, where there is neither being nor non-being, where others and self become empty, then one will be mentally and physically sublimated and will merge with the Tao in reality.

This is like wood and clay passing through fire to become charcoal and brick, never to decay.[160]

The rising of the sun ~ A story — *Contemporary*

A disciple said to his teacher: "Is there anything I can do to make myself enlightened?" The teacher replied: "As little as you can do to make the sun rise."

Shocked, the disciple said: "Then what use are the spiritual exercises you prescribe?"

Said the teacher: "To make sure you are not asleep when the sun begins to rise."[161]

Namdev *1270–1350*

When I see him, I sing – that's how this nothing of a slave became tranquil, patient: when you meet the radiance of the true master, you merge in song!

Where he makes the dazzling light visible, the unending sound rings out. Your light merges in the light – by the grace of the master I now know this.

The jewels in the lotus, his treasure house, glitter and flash like lightning. He is nearby, not far at all – permeating every part of you to the depths of your soul.

Where the unending sun shines, the burning of ceremonial lamps is neither here nor there – by the grace of the master I now know this.

Slave Namdev has merged in Tranquillity – singing, singing the sound, the song.[162]

Soami Ji of Agra

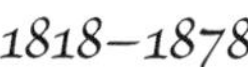

1818–1878

What a night!
What an incredible, amazing night.
I'm longing to tell someone –
But who will know what I'm talking about?
I saw, I tasted, the Root.
How to express it in words – this tremendous joy!
Earth and sky were alight with bliss,
Nectar poured from every particle of his body:
His feet – all it took was his feet
And darkness disappeared.

I saw him!
You think my eyes are glowing –
That's the radiance of his form.
Overwhelmingly attractive –
How not to surrender!
The trickle of nectar turned into a waterfall –
Hearing and seeing collected inside the clay pot,
Flew straight up to the skies of Trikuti:
Who could do that without a master?

I tasted the Root.
Earth and sky alight, nectar pouring – oh
Give up your self in surrender to the master today:
The deer will move back,
The doe will run away,
The ray will go straight for the centre of the sun
And soul will never fall again.

Radha Soami described everything,
Initiated me into the mysteries.
You won't catch me wandering
Away from his feet![163]

Odes of Solomon *100s–300s*

Draw for yourselves water from the living spring of the Lord – it has been opened to you! Come, all you who thirst, and drink it down, and rest beside the spring of the Lord.

Fair it is and pure, and gives rest to the soul. Sweeter by far than honey are its waters – the honeycomb of bees cannot be compared with it because it flows forth from the lips of the Lord, and from the heart of the Lord is its Name.

And it came unhindered and unseen: until it sprang up within them, people knew it not. Blessed are they who have drunk from it, and have found rest thereby.[164]

Juan de la Cruz *1542–1591*

On a night of darkness, enflamed by love and yearning – O happy chance! – I slipped away undetected, my house at last grown still.

Secure in the darkness, I climbed the secret ladder in disguise – chance taken, happily! – in darkness and concealment, my house lying quiet and still.

In that night of happiness, in secret, seen by no one and myself looking at nothing, with no other light or guide than the one burning in my heart: this light led me on more clearly than the midday sun to where he was waiting for me, the one I have known so intimately, in a place where no one could find us.

O night that guided me!
O night far sweeter than dawn!
O night that joined Beloved and lover –
Lover now transformed in Beloved!

He rested his head on my breast – blossoming! – kept entirely for him and him alone: and he slept, right there. And I caressed him, caressed as the breezes blew through the cedars, fanning him.

The breeze came from the merlon as I spread out his hair, and with his hand of serenity he wounded my neck, leaving all my senses suspended.

I stayed there, oblivious of myself, face leaning against the Beloved: everything ceased, self left behind, cares lost among the lilies, forgotten.[165]

Isaac Luria 1534–1572

It is impossible to write about mystical subjects because all things are connected with one another. I can hardly open up my mouth to speak without feeling as though the sea has burst its dams and overflowed. How then shall I express what my soul has received, and how can I put it down in a book?[166]

Kabir

1398–1518

After such a long time
I have got the Beloved.
Unbelievably lucky:
He has come to stay in my house!

I keep my mind absorbed
In the song of joy, ringing,
And I'm intoxicated,
Drinking down divine elixir.

My whole temple within
Is a blaze of light –
I lie sleeping here in his arms,
My darling, my Beloved.

I had a lot of disappointments,
Even despair, before this chance.
So where am I in this?
Beloved, it's all your grace!

Says Kabir, I did nothing:
Friends, God gave me union –
Fulfilled me for always with his bliss.
After such a long time
I have got the Beloved![167]

Moses Maimonides *1100s*

The individual's heart overflows with love as a result of his contemplation of God.

Extreme love, *mahabbah*, so that no thought remains that is directed toward a thing other than the Beloved, is passionate love, *ishk*.[168]

Jana *1263–1300s*

I eat God,
I drink God –
I sleep on God!

I give God,
I take God –
All I do: just God.[169]

Shams
1184–1247

Did you sleep in the morning so you could stay awake all night with the Beloved? When I want to be with my Beloved and have union with Him at night, I sleep in the daytime. But it matters not to Him. Once He comes, both sleep and thought will disappear, so even their trail of dust can no longer be seen.[170]

Rumi
1207–1273

Would I think of gardens, Beloved, with your face by my side? Would I long for light, Beloved, when I am lit by the fire of your love? They say sleep strengthens the mind – but does a lover need a mind?

I drank from his flaming cup and lost my mind. Now, like a moth, I'm circling around *shams,* the Sun.

Those beautiful words we said to one another are hidden in the secret heart of heaven. One day, like rain, they will pour our love story all over the world.[171]

Mira *1498–1573*

It's raining – make it pour!
Today my Lord has come
To my house –
He's here! Make it pour!

Small drops of rain
Gently falling,
Dense monsoon clouds overhead –
Make it pour!

The lakes were dry craters,
Cracked, deserted.
Now they're full, overflowing with joy:
My Lord has come to my home today!

I had to wait for so long.
But now I've got the Beloved –
He's mine!
Make it pour: My Lord has come home.

I can't help the fear in my heart
That he'll leave again.
Do we have to be apart?
But today he's home – make it pour!

Oh, Mira! He joined me to him
With a love so deep
We can never be separate again.
My Beloved – make it pour!

He was promised to me
At the beginning of time:
I've taken the Groom!
And he's here: Make it pour![172]

Sarmad *1590–1661*

My heart searched for your fragrance in the breeze moving at dawn; my eyes searched for the flower of your face in the garden of creation. Neither could lead me to your abode – contemplation alone showed me the way.[173]

Mechthild von Magdeburg *1207–1294*

That prayer has great power which a person makes with all his might. It draws down the great God into the little heart, it drives the hungry soul up into the fullness of God. It brings together two lovers, God and soul, in a wondrous place where they speak much of love.[174]

Kabir

1398–1518

Listen, dear friend:
Does my soul live in the Beloved
Or does he live in my soul?
I can't tell the difference
Between soul and Beloved –
Is it my soul or my Beloved in me?[175]

Caterina of Genoa

1447–1510

My "me" is God![176]

Téra... téra... téra... ~ A story

1500s

When he was a young man, the mystic Nanak worked in Sultanpur as a storekeeper in a granary, weighing out grain for sale.

One day, as he carefully weighed out the wheat, he reached *térah*, 'thirteen', and went on weighing kilo after kilo of wheat, punctuated by *téra... téra... téra...* ('yours, yours, yours') – immersed in ecstasy for the Beloved.[177]

Khusro *1253–1325*

I have become you,
You have become me:
I, the body – you, the soul.

From this outward difference
Let nobody say
I am other than you

Or you
Other
Than me.[178]

Bahu

1628–1691

A lover lost his heart to the Beloved
And while about it, lost himself too. *Lord...*

He was so totally lost
He didn't manage to turn back –
Happily confused in the one he loved,
He kept on going instead. *Beloved...*

Reason, intellect – forgot all about them:
Out of love, he merged
In the Beloved. *Lord...*

I'll sacrifice myself for anybody
In whom love has come to life
As passionately as this! *Beloved...*[179]

Gopi Chand's challenge ~ A story

100s BCE

In ancient times there was a king in the prime of life who renounced his throne – his power, his wealth, his land, his beautiful wives and palaces – all in search of enlightenment. His name was Gopi Chand.

As a challenge for his ego and his attachments, Gopi Chand's guru sent him as a mendicant to the capital of his old kingdom – to beg from the people he once ruled. Obeying his teacher, Gopi Chand walked hundreds of miles from the hills of Punjab all the way back to the kingdom in Bengal. Once there, he wandered the great capital city, begging as an ascetic – and sending to the guru whatever he received, through the disciples who had accompanied him.

Finally one day he ended up at the royal palaces. Word spread. The queens came running with gifts for the "mendicant," giving away their jewels and fine clothes since their husband, the king, was no longer with them. And then the excited chatter, the tears and the laughter quietened down as the gracious figure of Gopi Chand's mother appeared in the doorway.

Walking slowly down a garden path with Gopi Chand, she said, "Listen, jogi, you have renounced the world, and it isn't appropriate for a mere householder like me to preach to somebody like you. But you have come here begging alms, so we can offer you what we please. You don't keep any of the alms for yourself, so I shan't give you anything of that nature. Instead, I'm going to put three pieces of advice into your begging bowl. Listen well, dear jogi!

"First, live inside the strongest of strong forts.

"Second, eat nothing but the most delicious of good foods.

"Third, sleep at night on the softest and most comfortable of beds."

Gopi Chand was puzzled by her words. After a moment's reflection, he said: "Mother, it was your teaching that convinced me to become a renunciant. Now what is this upside-down advice you are giving me here? If it were any other woman, I would think she was mad! Where, mother, am I going to find strong forts and delicious food in the jungle? And soft beds? Out there we're lucky if we sleep on dry grass, with a few crumbs for our food!"

With a smile, the queen mother said, "Jogi, you haven't understood my meaning." When he asked her to explain, the queen mother said:

"What I mean is this – stay awake day and night meditating. When sleep completely overcomes you and you're exhausted, then fall asleep right where you are, whether it's sharp stones or lumps of clay. That is what I mean by the softest of beds: you will sleep better after spiritual effort than ever you did on a bed of rose petals!

"And as far as possible, eat less and remain hungry. When hunger makes it difficult to keep body and soul together, then have a bite to eat – tasteless dry bread or whatever is available. That's when a seven days' old dry husk will taste better than the sweetest dishes on the table of a king!

"As for living inside a strong fort: you have renounced a kingdom to become a yogi. Young women will come to you, older women and young girls too. No fort is stronger than the teacher's company. As long as you keep his company, remain under the mantle of his friendship, listen to his talks, you will be protected from all that. When you listen to the words of a saint, the mind is shamed and keeps to the straight path.

"There, that's all! These are the alms I'm putting into your begging bowl. Nothing else." And with a nod and a smile, the queen turned away from her son and went inside, over the threshold, into the palace.

The yogi bowed his thanks, and with a smile walked away through the palace grounds, out into the city, and onward, step by step, into the life unfolding before him.[180]

Chuang-tse *400s BCE*

The purpose of a rabbit snare is to catch rabbits. When the rabbits are caught, the snare is forgotten.

The purpose of words is to convey ideas. When the ideas are grasped, the words are forgotten.

Where can I find a man who has forgotten words? He is the one I would like to talk to![181]

PERSPECTIVE

Union, oneness, going home – on some level we relate to these long-forgotten spiritual states, and in quiet moments may long with a strange nostalgia.

A very small portion of mystic writings focuses on union. Mystics say that union, like love, is to be experienced, not talked about; once experienced, what can you say? When you are there, "you" are not; when you return to human consciousness, no words can begin to capture what you have experienced – nor can words make the experience accessible to others.

Unlike other traditions – of asceticism, renunciation and celibacy – the path towards union taught and practised by the mystics of the Naam bhakti tradition is based on a family life in the world. The lifestyle such mystics recommend encourages one to take care of family responsibilities and social obligations and to earn an honest income while also giving time to the spiritual practice. Ideally, this way of life is based on compassion, non-violence and love for all – a firm foundation for the inner practice, whose goal is union with the purest Essence.

The masters know from personal experience the challenges of being married, bringing up children, having a job, interacting socially – and they are proof that one can lead a caring family life while continuing to meet all one's spiritual commitments.

What we see in the mystics is that love for the One manifests as love for the many. The inner path towards realization of divine love leads to greater love in the world – the mystics' unconditional love and compassion for all living beings. There is no turning away from the world or renunciation and isolation; the mystics embrace the world and do whatever they can to help others. How can they do otherwise when they have reached the stage where they see only the Beloved in all!

Here and there the mystics give a glimmering, through metaphors and analogies, of what spiritual union is like.

Sometimes they describe the inner journey towards union, mentioning landmarks on the path and the increasing intoxication of the devotee, inwardly dancing, weeping or singing from ecstasy and love for the Beloved.

Frequently the bhakti mystics use the imagery of human love – husband/wife, lover/beloved – because this is familiar ground and it includes something of the intensity of the pleasure, passion and love play experienced within.

The ecstasy of these indescribable stages of divine union is hinted at in the songpoems of this section as bliss, amazement and gratitude. The context is spiritual experiences mentioned elsewhere in the mystic teachings: unearthly light, sounds and sights; the radiance of the Beloved; "sleeping" with the Beloved; his staying in one's "house" – all of it representing an inner merging of soul in Spirit that is beyond our understanding.

From the initial stages of effort, sacrifice and self-discipline to the later stages of purity, surrender and merging, the seeker gradually realizes there is nothing to distinguish lover and Beloved, individual and universal. There is and always has been no separation, no differentiation: only oneness. The essence grasped, words no longer serve, so the mystics fall silent.

Come, come, whoever you are –
Wanderer, worshipper, lover of leaving:
It doesn't matter,
Ours is a caravan of endless joy.
Even if you've broken your vows
  a thousand times –
Come, come, yet again come!

~ Rumi[182]

EXPLORATIONS

Glossary	185
Authors	189
Stories	194
Endnotes	195
Browsing	209
Spiritual research	211
Acknowledgements	213
Appreciation	217
Colophon	220

GLOSSARY

bhakti Devotion. *See also* **Naam bhakti tradition**

characteristics *prakritis:* twenty-five characteristics of mind and matter; the blueprint of the physical creation.

clay pot Large water pot made from unbaked clay (cheap, disposable); the body.

consciousness In the bhakti understanding, soul is consciousness – a drop of the ocean of consciousness, which is God. At the ordinary level of human experience, our consciousness is shrouded; we perceive very little beyond the physical surface. At the stage of full consciousness or realization, soul is free from its coverings (physical and mental) and attains to total consciousness. Mystics like Kabir, Nanak, Paltu, Tulsi of Hathras and Soami Ji of Agra use a special word for consciousness: *surat,* synonymous with attention, the soul's faculty of hearing, the soul.

darshan Seeing, beholding, gazing: looking at the master, inside oneself or outside, with attention so absorbed in the master that one is conscious of nothing else.

drowning Unrealized souls drown in the ocean of existence (rebirth); self-realization and God-realization are the solution.

eye centre Focal point in the forehead for meditation, also referred to by mystics in this book as the eye, heart, door of the heart, the tenth (door), sesame, merlon.

fire Divine love, inner light.

the five Five passions: lust, anger, greed, attachment, ego.

Friend The master, the Beloved, the Lord.

Great Darkness, Maha Sunn Spiritually evolved level of consciousness prior to God-realization.

gurmukh The guru or teacher; also, the devotee.

head Ego.

home Highest level of consciousness, also known as the home within the home (of the body), the home of love.

jogi Yogi. Occasionally used as affectionate term for the guru.

Maansarovar Inner landmark, threshold to the purely spiritual levels of realization; poetic name, "mountain lake".

master In the Naam bhakti tradition the mystic teacher is a living master who gives seekers the inner connection with Shabd or Naam and guides them to the highest levels of consciousness – self-realization and God-realization. Sufi terms: murshid, sheikh.

meditation A practice of inner focusing.

mind Bhakti mystics differentiate body *(tan)*, mind *(man)*, and soul *(rooh* or *aatma)* or consciousness *(surat)*. Mind is inanimate software: a tool, not an entity – powered and enlivened by the energy of soul; unenlightened mind is often identified with ego, I-ness, self.

mystic Generally speaking, a mystic is somebody who carries out an inner spiritual practice with the goal of realizing the inner mysteries. Mystics in different traditions adopt a wide range of methods and techniques to achieve their particular goals.

In the Naam bhakti tradition, the goal is self-realization and God-realization; the mystic (*sant,* saint) is a disciple who has achieved it.

While there may be several such bhakti mystics or fully realized disciples living unobtrusively here and there, the master is the one who has been appointed by his predecessor during his lifetime to carry on the onerous work of initiating seekers and providing inner and outer spiritual guidance.

Naam, the Name Divine power, one with God, that creates and sustains the universe; audible and visible within us as sound and light. It is also referred to by mystics as Spirit, Word *(shabd, kalma, logos)*, Great Mystery, Truth – among many other terms.

Naam bhakti tradition Various independent lines of mystics in India, traceable for several thousand years to present time – including masters from a variety of religious backgrounds – who practise and teach the way of attuning and then merging individual consciousness in the divine power they call Name or Word, Naam or Shabd.

name(s), repeating the name(s) *See* **simran**

pearl Realization, enlightenment.

radiant glory, radiant Beloved References to the astral or light form of the teacher, the radiant form.

regions, realms Levels of consciousness, accessible within through meditation; occasionally referred to as palaces ("going from palace to palace") or inner mansions.

saint, *sant* Fully realized mystic. *See* **mystic**

satguru True teacher.

satsang The master's company or discourse.

sesame *See* **eye centre**

séva Service of the master.

Shaah Rug Royal vein: Sufi term for the subtle central passageway leading beyond the eye centre.

Shabd Word, Sound: the divine energy that creates and sustains the universe, audible and visible within us as sound and light; also referred to by mystics in this book as the call, melody, unstruck unending sound, five sounds, sound current, the hymn, song, true song, song of the Spirits, song or voice of the Lord, unplayed music, tinkling of bells, the Thing, the essence, elixir, Tranquillity, serenity, the unspoken recitation, the unrepeatable name, the priceless goods, wealth, treasure, secret, All, Comforter, Truth, Spirit of Truth, Sat Shabd (true sound), Shabd of Satnaam (sound of true name). Same as Naam, the Name.

simran Remembrance, repetition: mental repetition of sacred names given by the spiritual teacher to initiates, sometimes referred to as continuous interior prayer; occasionally referred to as the mantra of the master.

songpoems *shabds:* The compositions of the pre-twentieth century bhakti mystics were usually passed on orally in the form of rhyming lyrics – shabds, designed for singing. They were easy for non-readers to memorize, sing and recite, and were composed in the ordinary spoken language of the region so anybody could understand.

Sunn Evolved spiritual level of consciousness.

Surat Shabd The Naam bhakti path: the merging of surat (consciousness) in Shabd (Word, Sound).

Tao Chinese Buddhist term – the way: undefinable absolute, nameless, beyond naming; openly associated by some Chinese mystics with the inner sound.

ten doors The eye centre (known as "the tenth") plus the nine outward openings of the body (eyes, ears, nostrils, mouth, two lower apertures).

Tranquillity Sahaj, the soul's natural state, the supreme level of consciousness; the state where the mind is in equipoise.

Trikuti Level of consciousness associated with the higher mind.

Turiya Superconsciousness.

the twenty-five *See* **characteristics**

unending unstruck sound *See* **Shabd**

waiting, watching Contemplating in meditation at the eye centre; also "gazing down the path": contemplating or gazing within.

AUTHORS

The IW *numbers are* ***endnote references*** *in the text, not page numbers.*

Abdisho Hazzaya (c.700) Christian; Syria. *IW* 33.
Abu Sa'id Ibn Abi'l Khayr (967–1049) Sufi; Iran. *IW* 38.
Angad (1504–1552) 1st successor of Nanak; Punjab, India. *IW* 150.
Ansari (1006–1088) Sufi; Afghanistan. *IW* 124.
Araqi or Iraqi, Fakhr ad-Din (1213–1289) Sufi; Iran. *IW* 80.
Arjan (1563–1606) 4th successor of Nanak; Punjab, India. *IW* 17, 52, 85.
Aseneth *See* ***Joseph and Aseneth***
Ibn Ata'illah (1200s–1309) Sufi; Egypt. *IW* 6.
Aurobindo (1872–1950) Teacher, Integral Yoga; India. *IW* 20, 45, 72, 89, 138.
Ba'al Shem Tov (1698–1760) Hasidic Judaism, Rabbi; Ukraine. *IW* 79.
Bahu (c.1628–1691) Sufi; Punjab. *IW* 117, 179.
Bassui Tokusho Zenji (1327–1387) Zen teacher; Japan. *IW* 9.
Bayazid Bastami (c.804–874) Sufi; Iran. *IW* 159.
Bhagavad Gita (c.5th–2nd BCE) Anonymous; Hindu scripture; India. *IW* 93.
Black Elk (1863–1950) Visionary, Oglala Lakota (Sioux); USA. *IW* 24.
Bonaventura (1221–1274) Franciscan visionary, cardinal; Italy. *IW* 73.
Book of Coming Forth into the Light (c.1700 BCE on) *rw nw prt m hrw*, often called *Book of the Dead*. Anonymous; incantations, prayers; Egypt. *IW* 111.

The Buddha (c.563–483 BCE) Teacher, Hindu; central figure in the Middle Way (Buddhism); India. *IW* 3, 56, 82.

Bullah (c.1680–1758) Sufi; Punjab, India. p.ix, *IW* 132.

Catarina of Genoa (1447–1510) Christian; Italy. *IW* 176.

Catarina of Siena (1347–1380) Dominican Order; Italy. *IW* 71.

Chödrön, Pema (1936–) Tibetan Buddhist nun; USA. *IW* 11, 50.

Chuang-tse (5th or 4th century BCE) Teacher, Taoism; China. *IW* 30, 44, 83, 98, 140, 181.

Yannus Chrysostomos (c.347–407) John Chrysostom: Christian, archbishop; Turkey. *IW* 86.

Cloud of Unknowing (1300s) Anonymous; Christian guide, contemplative prayer; England. *IW* 26, 88.

Confucius or **Kong-Qiu** (551–479 BCE) Philosopher; China. *IW* 30.

Dadu (c.1544–1603) Teacher, Muslim; India. *IW* 69, 121, 151.

David (c.1040–970 BCE) Hebrew, king of Judah. *IW* 115.

Desert Fathers (c.300 CE) Christian hermits and anchorites in Egypt, Palestine, Arabia and Iran. *IW* 29.

Dov Baer (c.1700–1772) Hasid, Rabbi; Ukraine. *IW* 58.

Eckhart (c.1250s–1329) Teacher, Dominican; Germany. *IW* 43, 134.

Eknath Easwaran (1910–1999) Writer; translator of ancient texts; teacher of Passage Meditation; India, USA. *IW* 56.

Epictetus (c.55–135) Stoic; Italy, Greece. *IW* 91.

Farid (c.1173–1265) Sufi; Punjab, India. p.viii, *IW* 47, 135.

François de Sales (1567–1622) Writer, bishop; France. *IW* 96.

Gobind Singh (1666–1708) 9th successor of Nanak; India. *IW* 155.

Gopi Chand (1st century BCE) Yogi; king of Bengal, India. *IW* 180.

Hadith Qudsi (c.7th century) Islamic tradition; sayings of God. *IW* 59.

Heard, Gerald (1889–1971) Writer, Ramakrishna Vedanta; UK, USA. *IW* 108.

Herrigel, Eugen (1884–1955) Philosopher, Zen practitioner; Germany. *IW* 46.

Inayat (1600s–1700s) Teacher, Muslim; Punjab, India. p.ix.

Iroquois legends Anonymous; Native American mystic wisdom. *IW* 110.

Isaiah (8th–7th centuries BCE) Prophet, Hebrew. *IW* 92, 127.

James (1st century CE) Younger brother and disciple of Jesus. *IW* 102.

Jami (1414–1492) Sufi; Iran. *IW* 107.

Jana (1263–1300s) Hindu, woman disciple of Namdev; India. *IW* 144, 169.

Jesus of Nazareth (c.6 BCE–c.34 CE) Teacher, Jewish; central figure in Christianity; Galilee. *IW* 21, 112, 122, 152.

Jilani (1077–1166) Sufi; Iran, Iraq. *IW* 35.

John (1st century CE) Writer, disciple of Jesus, Jewish; Galilee. *IW* 67, 145.

Joseph and Aseneth (c.200 CE) Anon; mystic allegorical story. *IW* 78, 141.

Juan de la Cruz (1542–1591) John of the Cross: Teacher, writer, reform Carmelite; Spain. *IW* 34, 106, 156, 165.

Julian of Norwich (c.1342–1416) Anchoress, Christian; England. *IW* 157.

Junayd (830–910) Sufi; Iraq. *IW* 25.

Kabir (c.1398–1518) Teacher, Muslim; India. p.x, *IW* 12, 28, 37, 99, 120, 139, 167, 175.

Kenzo, Awa (1880–1939) Zen practitioner; Japan. *IW* 46.

Khusro (1253–1325) Poet, Sufi; Delhi, India. *IW* 116, 137, 178.

Kook, Abraham Isaac (1865–1935) Writer, rabbi; Palestine. *IW* 31.

Lahiji, Shams ad-Din (c.1426–c.1506) Sufi; Iran. *IW* 40.

Lao-tse (6th century BCE?) Philosopher-author, *Tao Te Ching;* China. *IW* 44, 140.

Laurent de la résurrection (1614–1691) Brother Lawrence: Carmelite; France. *IW* 53, 130.

Law, William (1686–1761) Theologian, Christian; England. *IW* 131.

Lehna *See* **Angad**

Liu I-ming (c.1734–1836) Taoist, writer; China. *IW* 160.

Lull, Ramon (1233–1315) Writer, Christian missionary; Spain, Africa. *IW* 75, 114.

Luria, Isaac ben Solomon (1534–1572) Rabbi; Kabbalah; Palestine. *IW* 166.

Luther Standing Bear (1868–1939) Writer, Chief, Oglala Lakota (Sioux); USA. *IW* 4.

Maimonides, Moses (1100s) Jewish philosopher; Spain, Egypt. *IW* 168.

Mayorga, Nancy Pope (1904–1983) Writer, Ramakrishna Vedanta; USA. *IW* 54, 84, 108.

Mechthild (c.1207–1294) Writer, Christian; Germany. *IW* 63, 142, 174.

Mira (c.1498–1573) Poet, Hindu; Rajasthan, India. p.ix, *IW* 109, 125, 172.

The Mother (1878–1973) Teacher, Integral Yoga; India. *IW* 5, 61, 97, 123.

Namdev (1270–1350) Teacher, Hindu; Maharasthra and Punjab. *IW* 144, 162.

Nanak (1469–1539) Teacher, Hindu; central figure in Sikhism; Punjab, India. *IW* 66, 68, 150, 177.

Nasruddin (c.1300s?) Sufi figure, philosopher, wise man. *IW* 14.

Nizamuddin (1238–1325) Teacher, Sufi; Delhi, India. *IW* 137.

Odes of Solomon (c.1st 3 centuries CE) Anon Christian work. *IW* 164.

Paltu (1700s–1800s) Teacher, Hindu; Uttar Pradesh, India. p.x, *IW* 57, 81, 90, 147, 158.

Patmore, Coventry (1823–1896) Poet; England. *IW* 51.

Philo Judaeus of Alexandria (20 BCE–50 CE) Biblical philosopher, writer, Jewish; Egypt. *IW* 101.

Pinhas of Korets (1726–1791) Rabbi, Hasid; Ukraine. *IW* 95.

Plato (424–347 BCE) Writer, philosopher; Greece. *IW* 10, 39.

Prabhavananda (1893–1976) Monk, teacher, Ramakrishna Vedanta; India, USA. *IW* 84, 103.

Raleigh, Walter (1554–1618) Poet, soldier, explorer; England. *IW* 18.

Ramdas (1534–1581) 3rd successor of Nanak; Punjab, India. *IW* 128.

Ravidas (c.1414–1540) Teacher, Hindu; Uttar Pradesh and Rajasthan, India. *IW* 1, 74, 143.

Rinpoche, Trungpa (1939–1987) Tibetan Buddhist teacher; Tibet, UK, USA. *IW* 11.

Rumi (1207–1273) Sufi, scholar, poet, teacher; Turkey. *IW* 133, 149, 171, 182.

Sarmad (c.1590–1661) Poet, Jewish, Sufi; Iran, India. *IW* 173.

Sefer ha-bahir (1300s) Anon; Jewish mystic work; Kabbalah. *IW* 104.

Shah, Idries (1924–1996) Writer, publisher, Sufism; India, UK. *IW* 14.

Shams of Tabriz (1184–1247) Sufi, teacher; Iran, Turkey. *IW* 27, 48, 60, 65, 133, 136, 154, 170.

Shibli (c.861–946) Sufi; Iraq. *IW* 25.

Singh, Sawan (1858–1948) Teacher, Sikh; Punjab, India. *IW* 76, 120, 137, 180.

Soami Ji of Agra (1818–1878) Teacher, Hindu; Uttar Pradesh, India. *IW* 32, 62, 105, 163.

Socrates (469–399 BCE) Athenian philosopher, Plato's teacher; Greece. The Plato dialogues are attributed to Socrates. *IW* 10, 39.

Suzuki, Shunryu (1904–1971) Zen teacher; Japan, USA. *IW* 2.

Tagore, Rabindranath (1861–1941) Writer; Bengal, India. *IW* 16, 64.

Tegh Bahadur (1621–1675) 8th successor of Nanak; Punjab, India. *IW* 7, 94.

Tennyson, Alfred (1809–1892) Poet; England. *IW* 126.

Tersteegen, Gerhard (1697–1769) Teacher, Christian; Germany. *IW* 13, 23.

Thérèse de Lisieux (1873–1897) Carmelite nun; France. *IW* 118, 153.

Tohfah (800s) Woman Sufi; Syria. *IW* 119.

Tulsi of Hathras (1700s–1843) Teacher, Hindu; Uttar Pradesh, India. *IW* 22, 42, 77, 113.

Upanishads (c.650 to 400 BCE) Anon, Hindu; Sanskrit texts; India. *IW* 41, 70.

Yogananda (1893–1952) Teacher, Kriya Yoga, writer; India, USA. *IW* 93.

Zechariah (c.6th century BCE) Teacher, Hebrew; Judaea. *IW* 100.

STORIES

Ayaaz and the pearl (*Love*, IW 154) p.151
The beggar (*The Master*, IW 64) p.65
Bukhara and the drunkard (*The Master*, IW 76) p.74
A disciple complained (*Love*, IW 140) p.141
Donkey mind (*The Path*, IW 36) p.37
Earthquake (*The Path*, IW 46) p.45
Fierce dog (*Reality*, IW 11) p.16
Give what is yours (*The Master*, IW 68) p.68
Gopi Chand's challenge (*Union*, IW 180) p.176
Jana and Namdev (*Love*, IW 144) p.144
Joseph and Aseneth (*The Master*, *Love*, IW 78, 141) pp.76, 142
Kabir and the king of Bukhara (*Yearning*, IW 120) p.118
Letting go (*Reality*, IW 8) p.14
The modern disciple (*The Path*, IW 55) p.52
Nanak and Lehna (*Love*, IW 150) p.148
Nasruddin (*Reality*, IW 14) p.18
Nirvana (*Reality*, IW 3) p.12
Nizamuddin and Khusro (*Love*, IW 137) p.137
One penny (*Reality*, IW 15) p.18
The oyster and the pearl (*The Path*, IW 60) p.54
The rising of the sun (*Union*, IW 161) p.163
The rock (*The Mystery*, IW 87) p.89
Searching within (*The Master*, IW 79) p.77
The seeker's dream (*Reality*, IW 19) p.21
Téra... téra... téra... (*Union*, IW 177) p.174
True song (*The Mystery*, IW 110) p.103
What do you see in me? (*The Master*, IW 82) p.79
Yellow ribbons (*The Path*, IW 49) p.48

ENDNOTES

The oral tradition is a major source of compositions by most earlier mystics in India. For hundreds of years it was often the only source. Most of the Hindi/Punjabi books cited in the endnotes are not unique primary sources but are one of several published sources for the material; two exceptions to the rule are the Adi Granth and *Saar Bachan* (Soami Ji of Agra).

Commons as a source refers to stories passed on freely in the oral tradition, used as the basis for the version told here. Contemporary "commons" sources include talks, blogs and websites. **Permissions and publication data** Every effort has been made to obtain permission to reprint copyrighted material; for inadvertent omissions, please contact SRP.

Translations are by Anthea Guinness ("AG" in the endnotes) unless noted otherwise.

REALITY

1. Ravidas, "*ihu jag dukh ki khétari.*" English translation by AG. Hindi source: BP Sharma, *Sant Guru Ravidas Vani* (Surya, 1978), Sakhi 40.
2. Shunryu Suzuki Roshi cited in Pema Chödrön, *When Things Fall Apart* (Shambhala, 1997), p.43.
3. Buddhist tradition. Commons.
4. Luther Standing Bear, cited in Charles A Eastman Ohiyesa, "The Soul of the Indian," in Ray Berry, *Spiritual Athlete* (Joshua Press, 1993), p.163.
5. The Mother. Cf. *Collected Works of The Mother*, vol. 8, *Questions and Answers 1956* (Sri Aurobindo Ashram Press), p.402.
6. Ibn Ata'illah al-Iskandari, *Miftah al-Falah* (Key to salvation: a manual on zikr). English translator: not known.

7. Tegh Bahadur, "*jiu supana ar/u pékhana.*" English translation by AG. Punjabi source: Sri Guru Granth Sahib (Amritsar: SGPC), p.1427:23; referred to hereafter as Adi Granth.
8. Modern rendering of a traditional Sufi parable.
9. Bassui Zenji, cited in Philip Kapleau, *The Three Pillars of Zen* (Weatherhill, 1965), p.169.
10. Plato, *Republic* VII:514a+, dialogue between Socrates and Glaucon. Cf. Paul Shorey's translation in *The Collected Dialogues of Plato* (Princeton University Press, 1961; reprinted 1996).
11. Pema Chödrön, *When Things Fall Apart* (Shambhala, 1997), pp.29, 14–15, slightly abbreviated.
12. Kabir couplets, "*yaha to ghar hai prém ka, aaya prém kahaa~ gaya, prém bina dheeraj nahee~, jo deesai so to naahee~.*" English translation by AG first published in *L'Inconnu* magazine, 2008 (EMCI, Dakar, Senegal). Hindi sources: oral tradition; written sources include *Kabir Sakhi Sangrah* (Belvedere Printing Works – referred to hereafter as Belvedere – c.1902; 2000).
13. Gerhard Tersteegen, *The Quiet Way*, translated by Emily Chisholm (Epworth Press, 1950), cited in Nancy Pope Mayorga, "Gerhart Tersteegen," in *Spiritual Athlete* (Joshua Press, 1993), pp.74–75.
14. Idries Shah, *The Pleasantries of the Incredible Mulla Nasrudin* (Octagon Press); standard spelling for mullah and Nasruddin is used in this book.
15. Based on eye-witness accounts.
16. Rabindranath Tagore, *Gitanjali*, Song 38. First published in England in 1912, translated into English by Tagore himself from his Bengali version of *Gitanjali*; various English editions available, including Macmillan, 1971.
17. Guru Arjan, "*jis vakhar ka'u lain too aa'ia.*" English translation by AG first published in *L'Inconnu* magazine, 2010. Punjabi source: Adi Granth, p.283:15:5.
18. Walter Raleigh, "Even Such Is Time." Many variants of this poem (written c.1618) available in collections of Raleigh's writings.
19. Commons. Cf. Antony de Mello, *Song of the Bird* (Doubleday, 1984), pp.140–141.
20. Sri Aurobindo. Cf. *Sri Aurobindo Birth Centenary Library*, vols. 19 and 28, *The Life Divine* II:2:857 and *Savitri* I:42 (Sri Aurobindo Ashram Press).
21. New Testament, *Matthew* 6:22–23. English translation by AG from the Greek original. Cf. KJV (King James version), *Biblos Interlinear Bible, Strong's Concordance,* HELPS *Word-studies,* and Adam Clarke's *Commentary on the Bible* – for all of which, see BibleHub.com.

22. Tulsi of Hathras, "*dil ka hujra saaf kar.*" English translation by AG. Hindi sources: oral tradition; written sources include *Sant Bani* (Hemchand Bhargav), pp.44–45.
23. Gerhard Tersteegen, *The Quiet Way,* translated by Emily Chisholm (Epworth Press, 1950), cited in Nancy Pope Mayorga, "Gerhart Tersteegen," in *Spiritual Athlete* (Joshua Press, 1993), p.70.
24. Joseph Epes Brown, *The Sacred Pipe: Black Elk's Account of the Seven Rites of the Oglala Sioux* (University of Oklahoma Press, 1953), cited in Charles A Eastman Ohiyesa, "The Soul of the Indian," in Ray Berry, *Spiritual Athlete* (Joshua Press, 1993), p.165.
25. Junayd, "The pearl," translated by Andrew Harvey in *Perfume of the Desert* (Quest Books, 1999), p.19.
26. Anonymous, *The Cloud of Unknowing* (Penguin, 1978), p.109.
27. Shams of Tabriz. Cf. Farida Maleki, *Shams-e Tabrizi: Rumi's Perfect Teacher* (Science of the Soul Research Centre, 2011, hereafter referred to as SSRC), p.61:69.
28. Kabir, "*ham ghar jaara aapana.*" English translation by AG first published in *L'Inconnu* magazine, 2008. Hindi sources: oral tradition; written sources include *Kabir Sakhi Sangrah* (Belvedere, c1902; 2000).
29. *The Wisdom of the Desert: Some Sayings of the Desert Fathers* (Shambhala, 1994), translated by Thomas Merton.
30. Chuang-tse. Cf. Thomas Merton, *The Way of Chuang Tzu* (Shambhala, 2004), pp.55–56; James Legge, *Texts of Taoism* (Oxford University Press, 1891, "Sacred Books of the East" series, vols. 39–40), iv:1.
31. Abraham Isaac Kook, *Musar avikha*, p.93:4. Cf. Ben Zion Bokser's translation in *Jewish Mystical Tradition* (Pilgrim Press, 1981), p.267.

THE PATH

32. Soami Ji of Agra, "*guru kahé~ khol kar bhaa'i.*" English translation by AG. Hindi source: *Sar Bachan Radhaswami Nazam yani Chhand-Band* (Radha Soami Satsang Beas – hereafter referred to as RSSB – 1963), 20:10; abbreviated as *Saar Bachan.*
33. Abdisho Hazzaya. Cf. *Woodbrooke Studies: Christian Documents in Syriac, Arabic, and Garshuni,* edited and translated by Alphonse Mingana, Vol. 7: *Early Christian Mystics* (W Heffer & Sons, 1934).
34. John of the Cross. First selection: Prologue to *Ascent of Mount Carmel;* cf. Gerald Brenan, *St John of the Cross: His Life and Poetry* (Cambridge

University Press, 1973), p.110. Second selection: Excerpts from the poem *"Entréme donde no supe,"* English translation by AG.

35. 'Abd al-Qadir al-Jilani, *The Sublime Revelation (Al-Fath ar-Rabbani): A Collection of Sixty-two Discourses,* translated by Muhtar Holland (Al-Baz, 1996), pp.83, 201, 203.
36. Commons.
37. Kabir, *"khaalik khoobai khoob hai."* English translation by AG. Hindi sources: oral tradition; written sources include *Kabir Sahib ki Shabdavali* (Belvedere, c1902; 2000), 2:72.
38. Abu Sa'id Ibn Abi'l Khayr. Cf. "Spiritual Hunger," translated by Andrew Harvey in *Perfume of the Desert* (Quest Books, 1999), p.48.
39. Plato, *Republic* VII:514–516c, dialogue between Socrates and Glaucon. Cf. Paul Shorey's translation in *The Collected Dialogues of Plato,* edited by Edith Hamilton and Huntington Cairns (Princeton University Press, 1961; reprinted 1996).
40. Shams ad-Din Lahiji. Cf. "Give up your place," translated by Andrew Harvey, *Perfume of the Desert* (Quest Books, 1999), p.47.
41. *Mundaka Upanishad.* Cf. AK Ramanujan, *The Collected Essays of A.K. Ramanujan* (Oxford University Press, 1999), p.181.
42. Tulsi of Hathras, *"sun ai taqi na jaa'iyo zinhaar dékhna."* English translation by AG. Hindi sources: oral tradition; written sources include *Sant Bani* (Hemchand Bhargav), p.45.
43. Eckhart von Hochheim. Cf. Jonathan Star's adaptation of KO Schmidt, *Meister Eckhart's Way to Cosmic Consciousness,* translated by Léone Muller (1976), p.80, in *Two Suns Rising* (Bantam Books, 1992), p.160.
44. Chuang-tse. Cf. Thomas Merton, *The Way of Chuang Tzu* (Shambhala, 2004), pp.151–152; *Texts of Taoism* (Oxford University Press, 1891, Sacred Books of the East series, vols. 39–40), xiii:3–7.
45. Sri Aurobindo. Cf. *Sri Aurobindo Birth Centenary Library,* vols. 20 and 23, *The Synthesis of Yoga,* I and II:308–309 and *Letters on Yoga,* II and III:517 (Sri Aurobindo Ashram Press).
46. Cf. Eugen Herrigel, *The Method of Zen* (Routledge-Kegan, 1960), pp.11–12.
47. Farid couplets, *"kanDh/u kuhaaRa sir ghaRa, fareedaa~ chaar gavaa'ia hanDh kai, fareedaa~ dar darvési gaakhaRi."* English translation by AG first published in *RS Greetings* magazine (RSSB-A, Fayetteville, N. Carolina). Punjabi source: Adi Granth, pp.1377–1380:43, 2, 38.
48. Shams of Tabriz. Cf. *Shams-e Tabrizi* (SSRC, 2011), Farida Maleki translation, pp.144–145:128, 131.
49. A retelling of a traditional folk story cited in the *Reader's Digest* c1990.
50. Pema Chödrön, *When Things Fall Apart* (Shambhala, 1997), pp.144–145.

51. Coventry Patmore, "Psyche's Discontent" in *The Unknown Eros*, first published in 1877.
52. Guru Arjan, *"prabh kai simaran/i kaaraj pooré."* English translation by AG first published in *L'Inconnu* magazine, 2010. Punjabi source: Adi Granth, p.263:1:7.
53. Frère Laurent de la résurrection, *La pratique de la présence de dieu* (Brother Lawrence, *The Practice of the Presence of God*). Letter 2, translator not known; Cf. Cosimo Classics (2006) and the French original.
54. Nancy Pope Mayorga, *The Hunger of the Soul: A Spiritual Diary* (InnerQuest Publishing, 1995), December 2, 1952, p.8.
55. Commons.
56. *The Dhammapada*, 8:4:103. Cf. S Radhakrishnan (Oxford University Press, 1950) and Eknath Easwaran (Nilgiri Press, 2007).
57. Paltu, *"doosar palaTu ik raha."* English translation by AG. Cf. earlier version in *Saint Paltu* (RSSB, 1999), p.194. Hindi sources: oral tradition; written sources include *Paltu Sahib ki Bani* (Belvedere, c.1910; 1997), vol. 1, Kundli 164.
58. Dov Baer. Cf. Aryeh Kaplan, *Chasidic Masters* (Moznaim, 1989), p.37.
59. *Hadith Qudsi* ('sayings of God'): Islamic tradition.
60. Shams of Tabriz. Cf. *Shams-e Tabrizi* (SSRC, 2011), Farida Maleki translation, p.194:107.
61. The Mother. Cf. *Collected Works of The Mother*, vol. 9, *Questions and Answers 1957–58* (Sri Aurobindo Ashram Press), pp.419–421.

THE MASTER

62. Soami Ji of Agra, *"guru mohé apana roop dikhaao; dékh pyaaré mai~ samjhaa'oo~."* English translation by AG. Hindi source: *Saar Bachan* 33:15–16.
63. Mechthild of Magdeburg, *Das Fliessende Licht der Gottheit*. Cf. Lucy Menzies, *The Revelations of Mechthild of Magdeburg or The Flowing Light of the Divine Godhead* (Longmans, Green, 1953).
64. Rabindranath Tagore, *Gitanjali*, Song 50. First published in England in 1912, translated into English by Tagore himself from his Bengali version of *Gitanjali*; various English editions available, including Macmillan, 1971. 'Corn' in the fourth paragraph of Tagore's translation (UK English for wheat) has been rendered here 'wheat'.

65. Shams of Tabriz, *Shams-e Tabrizi* (SSRC, 2011), Farida Maleki translation, p.132:414.
66. Nanak, "*kavaN mool/u kavaN mat/i véla.*" English translation by AG. Punjabi source: Adi Granth, pp.942–943:43, 44.
67. New Testament, *John* 1:1–11. English translation by AG from the Greek original. Cf. KJV, *Biblos Interlinear Bible, Strong's Concordance,* HELPS *Word-studies.* Reference to *John* (1:6) is to John the Baptist, the master of Jesus, not John the author of the John Gospel.
68. Sikh tradition. Commons.
69. Dadu, "*niranjan jogi jaani lai chéla.*" English translation by AG. Hindi sources: oral tradition; written sources include *Dadu Dayal Granthavali,* ed. Parashuram Chaturvedi (Kashi Nagari Pracharini Sabha, samvat 2023), *Asavari,* p.405:17.
70. Anonymous, *Chandogya Upanishad,* vi:13. Cf. John Muir, *Metrical Translations from Sanskrit Writers* (1879), pp.247–248 FN; Swami Prabhavananda and Abbot George Burke, *The Chandogya Upanishad,* ocoy.org; translations of Swami Nikhilananda, Robert Ernest Hume, Swami Swahanand, Dominic Goodall. My thanks to Sankar Narayanan for help finalizing the translation.
71. Raymond of Capua, *The Life of St. Catherine of Siena,* translated by George Lamb (PJ Kenedy, 1960), cited in Carol Lee Flinders, *Enduring Grace* (HarperCollins, 1993), p.110.
72. Sri Aurobindo. Cf. *Sri Aurobindo Birth Centenary Library,* vol. 20, *The Synthesis of Yoga,* I and II (Sri Aurobindo Ashram Press), pp.60–61.
73. Bonaventure, *The Mystical Vine* (Fleur de lys, 1955?).
74. Ravidas couplets, "*ravidaas so'i saadhoo bhalo*" (2x), "*saadh sangat/i poonji bha'i.*" English translation by AG. Hindi sources: *Ravidas Darshan* (Sri Guru Ravidas Sansthan, 1973), pp.89, 90, and BP Sharma, *Sant Guru Ravidas Vani* (Surya, 1978), p.8.
75. Ramon Lull, *The Book of the Lover and the Beloved* (1283). Cf. E Allison Peers, translation from the Catalan (Macmillan, 1923).
76. Commons. Cf. Sawan Singh, story told in Punjabi satsangs; English version by AG with inputs from CF Wordsworth. For a collection of other stories told by Sawan Singh, see *Parmaarthi Saakhiyaa~* (RSSB, 1964) and *Tales of the Mystic East* (RSSB).
77. Tulsi of Hathras, "*aré ai taqi takté raho.*" English translation by AG. Hindi sources: oral tradition; written sources include *Sant Bani* (Hemchand Bhargav), p.46.
78. Excerpts from *Joseph and Aseneth,* cited in full in John Davidson, *The Divine Romance: Tales of an Unearthly Love* (SSRC); cf. p.128.

79. A Hasidic parable told in the 1700s by the Ba'al Shem Tov. Oral tradition. Cf. the version told by his successor, Ya'akov Yosef, in Rachel Elior, *The Mystical Origins of Hasidism*, translated from the Hebrew *Herut al-haluhot* by Shalom Carmi (Littman Library of Jewish Civilization, 2006), p.75.
80. Fakhr ad-Din Araqi, *La'amat* ('divine flashes') 27, translated by Shahram Shiva and Jonathan Star in *Two Suns Rising* (Bantam Books, 1992), p.138.
81. Paltu, "*seetal chandan chandrama*." English translation by AG. Hindi sources: oral tradition; written sources include *Paltu Sahib ki Bani* (Belvedere, c.1910; 1997), vol. 1, Kundli 23.
82. Commons.
83. Chuang-tse. Cf. Thomas Merton, *The Way of Chuang Tzu* (Shambhala, 2004), pp.103–104; *Texts of Taoism* (Oxford University Press, 1891, "Sacred Books of the East" series, vols. 39–40), xvii:3.
84. Nancy Pope Mayorga, *The Hunger of the Soul: A Spiritual Diary* (InnerQuest Publishing, 1995), January 5, 1968, p.109: excerpt from an interview with her teacher.

THE MYSTERY

85. Guru Arjan, "*saajan sant karahu ihu kaam/u*." English translation by AG. Punjabi source: Adi Granth, p.290:20:5.
86. John Chrysostom, cited in the anonymous work of a Russian pilgrim, *The Way of a Pilgrim*.
87. Commons.
88. Anonymous, *The Cloud of Unknowing*. Translator: not known.
89. Sri Aurobindo. Cf. *Sri Aurobindo Birth Centenary Library*, vol. 23, *Letters on Yoga*, II and III (Sri Aurobindo Ashram Press), pp.925–926.
90. Paltu, "*naam naam sab kahat hai~*." English translation by AG. Hindi sources: oral tradition; written sources include *Paltu Sahib ki Bani* (Belvedere, c.1910; 1997), vol. 1, Kundli 11.
91. Epictetus, *The Discourses*. Translated in *God of a Hundred Names*, Barbara Greene and Victor Gollancz, editors (Victor Gollancz Ltd, 1966), p.241.
92. Bible, *Isaiah* 26:19, 30:29–30. Cf. KJV.
93. Yogananda, *Man's Eternal Quest: Collected Talks and Essays* (Self-Realization Fellowship, 1982).

94. Tegh Bahadur, "*naam/u rahio saadhoo rahio.*" English translation by AG. Punjabi source: Adi Granth, p.1429:56.
95. Pinhas Shapiro of Korets, *Sefer midrash Pinhas* or 'book of Pinhas's commentary', p.10, in Zalman Schachter-Shalomi, *Spiritual Intimacy* (Jason Aronson, 1991), p.149.
96. Francis de Sales, *On Meditation*. Translator: not known.
97. The Mother. Cf. *Collected Works of The Mother*, vol. 9, *Questions and Answers 1957–58*, pp.414–416; vol. 8, *Questions and Answers 1956*, pp.172–174; vol. 7, *Questions and Answers 1955*, pp.195–196 (Sri Aurobindo Ashram Press).
98. Chuang-tse. Cf. Thomas Merton, *The Way of Chuang Tzu* (Shambhala, 2004), pp.131–133; *Texts of Taoism* (Oxford University Press, 1891,"Sacred Books of the East" series, vols. 39–40), xx:2.
99. Kabir, "*kabeer adhi saakh koTh granth ko jaan.*" English translation by AG. Hindi sources: oral tradition; written sources include *Kabir Sakhi Sangrah* (Belvedere, c.1902; 2000). Minor text variations: "*kul granth*" or "*koTh granth.*"
100. Bible, *Zechariah* 14:9. Cf. Masoretic Hebrew text and the JPS 1917 edition.
101. Philo Judaeus of Alexandria, *Allegorical Interpretation* III:59. Cf. John Davidson, *The Divine Romance* (SSRC), p.145, referring to the translations of EH Colson and GH Whitaker and of GRS Mead.
102. New Testament, *James* 1:22. English translation by AG from the Greek original. Cf. KJV, *Biblos Interlinear Bible, Strong's Concordance.*
103. Prabhavananda, cited in Nancy Pope Mayorga, *The Hunger of the Soul: A Spiritual Diary* (InnerQuest Publishing, 1995), 1968–1969, pp.115, 109.
104. *Sefer ha-bahir* ('book of brilliance'), no.22. Cf. Aryeh Kaplan, *The Bahir: Illumination* (Samuel Weiser, 1979).
105. Soami Ji of Agra, "*ghaT jhum rahi ab surat rangeeli.*" English translation by AG. Hindi source: *Saar Bachan* 35:19.
106. John of the Cross, *Spiritual Canticle*. Cf. Kieran Kavanaugh OCD and Otilio Rodriguez OCD in *The Collected Works of St. John of the Cross* (Institute of Carmelite Studies).
107. Nur ad-Din 'Abd ar-Rahman Jami, *Diwaan-e Jami*. Translator: not known; with thanks to Bill Self for the quote.
108. Nancy Pope Mayorga, *The Hunger of the Soul: A Spiritual Diary* (InnerQuest Publishing, 1995), December 29, 1966, p.107.
109. Mira, "*paayo ji mai~ to naam ratan dhan paayo.*" English translation by AG. Hindi sources: oral tradition; written sources include *Mirabai ki Shabdavali* (Belvedere c.1902; 2000).

110. Haudenosaunee legend (the Iroquois of the northeastern USA). Cf. Michael Parents version, *Time* magazine (31 August 1981).

111. *Book of Coming Forth into the Light,* often called *The Book of the Dead.* Cf. EA Wallis Budge, *From Fetish to God in Ancient Egypt* (Oxford University Press, 1934), Appendix, nos. 2, 5–7.

112. New Testament, *John* 14:16–18. English translation by AG from the Greek original. Cf. KJV, *Biblos Interlinear Bible, Strong's Concordance,* HELPS *Word-studies.*

YEARNING

113. Tulsi of Hathras, *"jin piy ki birha basai."* English translation by AG. Hindi sources: oral tradition; written sources include *Tulsi Sahib ki Shabdavali* (Belvedere, c.1905; 2000), vol. 1:91.

114. Ramon Lull, *The Book of the Lover and the Beloved* (1283). Cf. E Allison Peers, translation from the Catalan (Macmillan, 1923).

115. Bible, *Psalm* 119:147–148. Cf. KJV and *Aramaic Bible in Plain English.*

116. Khusro, *"gori sové séj par."* English translation by AG. Hindi sources: oral tradition; written sources include ektaramusic.com/ak/urs.html.

117. Bahu, *"jo dil mangé hové naahee~,"* Bait 49. English translation by AG. Punjabi sources: oral tradition; written sources include *Abyat-i-Bahu* (Altaf Ali, ed., 1975) and *Kalam-i-Sultan Bahu* (Nazir Ahmad, ed.).

118. Thérèse of Lisieux, from *L'histoire d'une âme,* posthumous collection of her writings translated into English by John Clarke OCD as *Story of a Soul: The Autobiography of St. Thérèse of Lisieux* (Institute of Carmelite Studies, 1977), p.178.

119. Tohfah of Syria. Cf. "In the Dust," translated by Andrew Harvey in *Perfume of the Desert* (Quest Books, 1999), p.93.

120. Commons. Cf. Sawan Singh, *"bukhaare da baadshaah."* English version by AG. Punjabi source: *Parmaarthi Saakhiyaa~* (RSSB, 1964); for collected stories in English, see *Tales of the Mystic East* (RSSB).

121. Dadu, *"ajahu na nikasé praan kaThor."* English translation by AG. Hindi sources: oral tradition; written sources include *Dadu Dayal Granthavali,* ed. Parashuram Chaturvedi (Kashi Nagari Pracharini Sabha, samvat 2023), *Gauri* 5, p.310.

122. New Testament, *John* 16:21–22. English translation by AG from the Greek original. Cf. KJV, *Biblos Interlinear Bible, Strong's Concordance,* HELPS *Word-studies.*

123. The Mother. Cf. *Collected Works of The Mother*, vol. 4, *Questions and Answers 1950–51*, pp.18–19; vol. 9, *Questions and Answers 1957–58*, pp.135–136 (Sri Aurobindo Ashram Press).
124. Abdullah Ansari of Herat, from *Munajat* ('intimate conversations' or prayers to God). Cf. *God of a Hundred Names*, Barbara Greene and Victor Gollancz, editors (Victor Gollancz Ltd, 1966), p.231.
125. Mira, "*jogiya ji nisadin jo'oo~ baaT.*" English translation by AG first published in *L'Inconnu* magazine, 2009. Hindi sources: oral tradition; written sources include *Mira Brahat Padavali* (Rajasthan Oriental Research Institute, 1968–1975), vol. 1.
126. Alfred Tennyson, *In Memoriam A.H.H.*, from canto 54. *The Works of Alfred, Lord Tennyson, Annotated* (The Eversley Edition), 9 vols.
127. Bible, *Isaiah* 30:19–21. Cf. *Tanakh: The Holy Scriptures.*
128. Ramdas, "*har/i darsan ka'u méra man/u bahu taptai.*" English translation by AG. Punjabi source: Adi Granth, p.861:4:6.
129. Ancient Egyptian, 13th century BCE. Cf. JH Breasted, quoted in *God of a Hundred Names*, Barbara Greene and Victor Gollancz, editors (Victor Gollancz Ltd, 1966), p.235.
130. Frère Laurent de la résurrection, *La pratique de la présence de dieu* (Brother Lawrence, *The Practice of the Presence of God*), Letters 14, 12. Cf. the Epworth Press edition (1932–1948).
131. William Law, cited by Nancy Pope Mayorga in *The Hunger of the Soul: A Spiritual Diary* (InnerQuest Publishing, 1995), p.5.
132. Bullah, "*kadi aa mil biraho~ sataa'i noo~.*" English translation by AG. Punjabi sources: oral tradition; written sources include *Kulliyat-i Bulleh Shah* (Faqir Muhammad).
133. Shams of Tabriz. Cf. *Shams-e Tabrizi* (SSRC, 2011), Farida Maleki translation, p.270:260. Shams quotes his disciple, Rumi – whose poem refers to Shams!
134. Eckhart von Hochheim, in *God of a Hundred Names*, Barbara Greene and Victor Gollancz, editors (Victor Gollancz Ltd, 1966), p.165.

LOVE

135. Farid couplets, "*fareedaa~ galee'é chikkaR/u door ghar/u, bheeja'u seeja'u kambali.*" English translation by AG, first published in *RS Greetings* magazine (RSSB-A, Fayetteville, N. Carolina). Punjabi source: Adi Granth, p.1379:24–25.

136. Shams of Tabriz. Cf. *Shams-e Tabrizi* (SSRC, 2011), Farida Maleki translation, pp.232–233:628, 660.
137. Commons. Cf. Sawan Singh, *"peer di jutti da mull."* English version by AG. Punjabi source: *Parmaarthi Saakhiyaa~* (RSSB, 1964); for collected stories in English, see *Tales of the Mystic East* (RSSB). Kabir verse quoted by Sawan Singh is from Kabir's *saakhis*.
138. Sri Aurobindo. Cf. *Sri Aurobindo Birth Centenary Library*, vol. 23, *Letters on Yoga*, II and III (Sri Aurobindo Ashram Press), pp.776, 780.
139. Kabir couplets, *"kabeer baadal prém ko, jab mai~ tha tab guru nahee~, méra mujh mé~ kachhu nahee~, aaTh jaam chausaThi ghaRi."* English translation by AG. Hindi sources: oral tradition; written sources include *Kabir Sakhi Sangrah* (Belvedere, c.1902; 2000).
140. Chuang-tse. Cf. Thomas Merton, *The Way of Chuang Tzu* (Shambhala, 2004), pp.148–154; *Texts of Taoism* (Oxford University Press, 1891, "Sacred Books of the East" series, vols. 39–40), xxiii:3–7.
141. Excerpt from *Joseph and Aseneth*, cited in full in John Davidson, *The Divine Romance: Tales of an Unearthly Love* (SSRC), p.157.
142. Mechthild of Magdeburg, *Das Fliessende Licht der Gottheit* (3:5). Cf. Lucy Menzies, *The Revelations of Mechthild of Magdeburg or The Flowing Light of the Divine Godhead* (Longmans, Green, 1953).
143. Ravidas, *"ja'u ham baandhé moh phaas."* English translation by AG. Hindi source: Adi Granth, p.658:4:2.
144. Commons. Thanks to Judith Sankaranarayan and Maggie Segal.
145. New Testament, *1 John* 4:8. English translation by AG from the Greek original. Cf. *Biblos Interlinear Bible, Strong's Concordance.*
146. Anonymous, 13th-century German. English translation by AG with helpful inputs from Margaret Humbert-Droz.
147. Paltu, *"prém divaana man yaar."* English translation by AG. Hindi sources: oral tradition; written sources include *Paltu Sahib ki Bani* (Belvedere, c.1910; 2000), vol. III, Shabd 49.
148. Unknown psalmist. Bible, *Psalm* 69:9. Cf. KJV, *Biblos Interlinear Bible,* Strong's *Concordance.*
149. Jalal ad-Din Rumi, couplets from the *Diwan-e Shams-e Tabrizi*. Cf. Maryam Mali and Azima Melita Kolin, *Rumi: Gardens of the Beloved* (Element/HarperCollins, 2003), pp.73, 109, 133.
150. Sikh tradition. Commons.
151. Dadu couplets, *"jab lag sees na saumpiyé, daadu pyaala noor da, jo kuchh diya hamkau~, aasik maasuk hvai gaya."* English translation by AG. Hindi sources: oral tradition; written sources include *Dadu Dayal*

ki Bani (Belvedere, 2 vols., c.1905; 1963–1974), vol. I, *Biraha* 61, *Parcha* 241, *Biraha* 42, 147.

152. New Testament, *Matthew* 5:8. KJV.
153. Thérèse of Lisieux from *L'histoire d'une âme,* posthumous collection of her writings translated into English by John Clarke OCD as *Story of a Soul: The Autobiography of St. Thérèse of Lisieux* (Institute of Carmelite Studies, 1977).
154. Shams of Tabriz. Cf. *Shams-e Tabrizi,* translated by Farida Maleki (SSRC, 2011), pp.190–192:87–9. As told by Shams, the story is a metaphor for the love of Shams and his disciple Rumi; the final verse expresses Shams's total focus on Rumi.
155. Gobind Singh, *"saach kahoo~ sun lého sabhee."* English translation by AG. Punjabi source: Dasam Granth 14:9:29.
156. John of the Cross, *"Tras de un amoroso lance."* English translation by AG. Cf. Lynda Nicholson's English rendering in *St John of the Cross* (Cambridge University Press, 1973), pp.175, 177.
157. Julian of Norwich, *Showings,* Long Text 5. Cf. translation by Edmund Colledge OSA and James Walsh SJ (Paulist Press, 1978).

UNION

158. Paltu, *"phirai ik jogi nagar bhulaana."* English translation by AG. Hindi sources: oral tradition; written sources include *Paltu Sahib ki Bani* (Belvedere, c.1910; 2000), vol. III, Shabd 129.
159. Bayazid Bastami, "No trace or sign," cited by Andrew Harvey in *Perfume of the Desert* (Quest Books, 1999), p.149.
160. Liu I-ming, "Wood and Charcoal, Clay and Brick" in *Awakening to the Tao,* translated by Thomas Cleary (Shambhala, 1988), p.16.
161. Cf. Anthony de Mello, *One Minute Wisdom* (Image, 1988).
162. Namdev, *"jab dékha tab gaava."* English translation by AG. Punjabi source: Adi Granth, pp.656–657:1.
163. Soami Ji of Agra, *"mangal mool aaj ki rajni."* English translation by AG. Hindi source: *Saar Bachan* 37:26.
164. Cf. *The Odes of Solomon: Mystical Songs from the Time of Jesus,* ed. John Davidson (SSRC), 30:1–7, p.134.
165. John of the Cross, *"En una noche oscura."* English translation by AG. Cf. *Spiritual Link* magazine (SSRC, November 2005, p.20), translator not known; Lynda Nicholson, *St John of the Cross* (Cambridge University

Press, 1973, pp.145, 147); and Nancy Pope Mayorga, "St John of the Cross" (in *Spiritual Athlete*, Joshua Press, 1993, pp.150–151).

166. Isaac ben Solomon Luria, *Likutei shas* (Livorno, 1790), 3c. Cf. translation of Lawrence Fine, *Safed Spirituality* (Paulist Press, 1984), p.62.
167. Kabir, "*bahut dinan thai~ mai~ preetam paayé.*" English translation by AG. Hindi sources: oral tradition; written sources include *Kabir Sahib ki Shabdavali* (Belvedere, c.1902; 2000).
168. Moses Maimonides, *Mishneh torah, yesodei ha-torah*, 2:2, translated in Aryeh Kaplan, *Meditation and the Bible* (Weiser Books, 1978), p.120. Moses Maimonides, *Guide of the Perplexed*, translation by Shlomo Pines (University of Chicago Press, 1963), II:627.
169. Janabai. Marathi sources: oral tradition; written sources include *Sant Vachanamrit* compiled by R Ranade (Shri Gurudev Ranade Samadhi Trust, 1986), p.148:23. Cf. *Many Voices, One Song: The Poet Mystics of Maharashtra*, translated by Judith Sankaranarayan (RSSB, 2013), p.25.
170. Shams of Tabriz, *Shams-e Tabrizi* (SSRC, 2011), Farida Maleki translation, p.168:654.
171. Jalal ad-Din Rumi, couplets from the *Diwan-e Shams-e Tabrizi*. Cf. Maryam Mali and Azima Melita Kolin in *Rumi: Gardens of the Beloved* (Element/HarperCollins, 2003), pp.141, 206, 221.
172. Mira, "*méha barsavo karé ré.*" English translation by AG first published in *L'Inconnu* magazine, 2009. Hindi sources: oral tradition; written sources include *Mira Sudha Sindhu* (Shri Mira Prakashan Samiti, 1957), p.441.
173. Sarmad. Cf. *Sarmad, Martyr to Love Divine* (RSSB, 2005).
174. Mechthild of Magdeburg, *Das Fliessende Licht der Gottheit* (5:13). Cf. Lucy Menzies, *The Revelations of Mechthild of Magdeburg or The Flowing Light of the Divine Godhead* (Longmans, Green, 1953).
175. Kabir, "*sunu sakhi pee'a mahi jee'u basai.*" English translation by AG. Hindi sources: oral tradition; written sources include *Kabir Sakhi Sangrah* (Belvedere, c.1902; 2000).
176. Catherine of Genoa, quoted in Carol Lee Flinders, *Enduring Grace* (HarperCollins, 1993), p.xxii.
177. Sikh tradition. Commons.
178. "*man tu shudam,*" much-quoted verse in Persian by Khusro of Delhi. English translation by AG. Persian source: oral tradition.
179. Bahu, "*aashiq shahu dé dil khaRaa'ia,*" Bait 136. English translation by AG. Punjabi sources: oral tradition; written sources include *Abyat-i-Bahu* (Altaf Ali, ed., 1975) and *Kalam-i-Sultan Bahu* (Nazir Ahmad, ed.).

180. Commons. Cf. Sawan Singh, "*maa~ di sikkhiaa~*." English version by AG. Punjabi source: *Parmaarthi Saakhiyaa~* (RSSB, 1964); for collected stories in English, see *Tales of the Mystic East* (RSSB).

181. Chuang-tse. Thomas Merton, *The Way of Chuang Tzu* (Shambhala, 2004), p.179; *Texts of Taoism* (Oxford University Press, 1891, "Sacred Books of the East" series, vols. 39–40), xxvi:11.

THE INNER WAY

182. Cf. RA Nicholson's translation of Jalal ad-Din Rumi.

THE WAY IT IS

183. Anonymous, 14th-century English. Modern English rendering by AG.

BROWSING

Whatever one's background, books by followers of any tradition provide fascinating insights and encouragement for one's own explorations and practice. In that spirit a few books are listed here, whose authors include a range of religious backgrounds: Buddhist, Christian, Hindu, Islamic, Jewish, Mayan, non-denominational and Universalist.

- **Anonymous** 19th-century Russian writer (Eastern Orthodox Christian mysticism) *The Way of a Pilgrim* (*Récits d'un pèlerin russe*).
- **Miriam Bokser Caravella** (mystic tradition and Judaism) *The Mystic Heart of Judaism.*
- **Pema Chödrön** (American Buddhist nun; Chögyam Trungpa) *When Things Fall Apart: Heart Advice for Difficult Times;* also *Start Where You Are.*
- **AS Dalal** (Hinduism, Integral Yoga) *Growing Within: The Psychology of Inner Development – Selections from the Works of Sri Aurobindo and The Mother,* and other books on Integral Yoga.
- **John Davidson** (mystic tradition and Christianity) *The Divine Romance: Tales of an Unearthly Love* and other books on the origins of Christianity, including *The Gospel of Jesus;* also *A Treasury of Mystic Terms* (multi-volume), and a series of books on science and mysticism: *One Being One* and *Subtle Energy,* among others.

- **Eknath Easwaran** (Passage Meditation, founder of the Blue Mountain Center of Meditation) Translations and introductions to the *Bhagavad Gita,* the *Dhammapada,* the *Upanishads;* books on Passage Meditation and the Eight Point Program.
- **Carol Lee Flinders** (Passage Meditation; Eknath Easwaran) *At the Root of This Longing: Reconciling a Spiritual Hunger and a Feminist Thirst;* also *Enduring Grace: Living Portraits of Seven Women Mystics.*
- **Andrew Harvey** (Sacred Activism) *Perfume of the Desert: Inspirations from Sufi Wisdom* and other books.
- **Jack Kornfield** (Insight Meditation; Ajahn Chah) *A Path with Heart: A Guide through the Perils and Promises of Spiritual Life;* also *After the Ecstasy, the Laundry* and *Teachings of the Buddha.*
- **Shraddha Liertz** (Benedictine nun and mystic tradition) *Adventure of Faith.*
- **Nancy Pope Mayorga** (Ramakrishna Vedanta meditation; Swami Prabhavananda) *The Hunger of the Soul: A Spiritual Diary.*
- **Thomas Merton** (Trappist monk) *The Way of Chuang Tzu;* also *Seven Storey Mountain,* and many other books.
- **Martín Prechtel** (Mayan Shaman healer; Nicolas Chiviliu Tacaxoy) *Secrets of the Talking Jaguar: Memoirs from the Living Heart of a Mayan Village.*
- **Muhyiddin Shakoor** (Sufi; Sheikh Sayyid Ahmed ar-Rufai) *The Writing on the Water: Chronicles of a Seeker on the Islamic Sufi Path.*
- **Jonathan Star** (Siddha Yoga; Gurumayi) *Two Suns Rising: An Anthology of Eastern and Western Mystical Writings.*
- **Tom Owen-Towle** (Unitarian Universalism) *Freethinking Mystics with Hands: Exploring the Heart of Unitarian Universalism.*

SPIRITUAL RESEARCH

Mystic writings may inspire one with a desire to have a spiritual practice and a genuine spiritual guide. Several questions naturally arise: Is every spiritual teacher a true master? Is every mystic capable of being an inner guide? Is every "mystic practice" part of the true way? Can one follow a spiritual path on one's own, without an expert guide?

We are graced with inquiring minds and a need to be intellectually satisfied. There is no reason to settle for anything less. The following points, culled from the talks and writings of the mystics, may help as reminders and touchstones at any time in our life.

True masters always live the path they teach. They do not claim that the path they follow is the only way and they encourage seekers to research thoroughly before making a commitment. They do not sit in judgement on any other teacher or any other teaching. They seek no mundane advantage from their work. For them, the sharing of truth is not a commercial transaction; they do not charge money, whether for giving talks or for passing on the inner practice.

True masters are willing to answer a seeker's questions but make no attempt to persuade, reminding seekers that conviction must come from within, not through words or emotions. They behave in private and in public with complete integrity. They use donations in the service of others, providing for their own needs from their own honestly earned family income.

Do such teachers exist? Yes. But the bottom line is that most of us are not evolved enough to differentiate a true master from a teacher of lesser spiritual standing. How can a child in kindergarten have any idea of the academic level attained by her teacher? When in doubt, one needs to go on looking. Sincerity, longing, searching – these are what count. As a seeker, it is entirely appropriate to ask questions about the practice and the path one is interested in, to air one's doubts and to study carefully any books about the path.

A contemporary mystic says: If you spend your whole life in spiritual research, it is not time wasted, it is time gained. When your intellect is satisfied, you will move forward without hesitation on your spiritual journey.

ACKNOWLEDGEMENTS

Polished by a hundred hands...

I feel deep gratitude for my teachers – and for supportive friends, family and colleagues. It is a pleasure to acknowledge a few by name; I thank also the ones not named here – including the colleagues who made allowances for growing pains and worked with me so tolerantly throughout my early years in India.

Much appreciation to Faith Singh, whose bhakti assignment in 2010 unexpectedly morphed into Salt River books.

And to my sister Chloe Faith Wordsworth: she came in at key moments with significant suggestions and used this book in its various incarnations the moment she got a copy.

Many thanks to the people who read the book, partially or as a whole, giving helpful feedback. *The early version:* Cindy Rawlinson; Margaret Humbert-Droz, Lindis Guinness, Farida Sharan, Janni Brenn, Carole Thelin, Irving Raimi, Connie Rawlinson, Cyndi Toschik, Greg Meyer. *And the recent version:* Berkeley Digby; Paul Moore, Cindy Rawlinson, Ken Frĕad, Barbara Merritt, Connie Rawlinson, Michelle Bongiorno, Jan Jones.

To Renu Bhagat, who checked the bhakti translations against the Hindi/Punjabi – and is not to be blamed for the times I pushed conventional meaning. And to Carol White, designer of books, for her design ideas and careful work – and for that elegant Salt River logo!

Much appreciation for their willing assistance with other aspects of the project: Maggie Segal; Lee Arnon, Miriam Bokser Caravella, Gaurav Chawla, Harmesh Clair, Rune Clausen, John Davidson, Parmanand Desai, Nirmal Dhesi, Rebecca Hammons, Philippe Julien, Sophia Latifi, Terry Levitan, Farida Maleki, Ann Marshall, Rajni Mirchandani, Ron Morey, Sankar Narayanan, Peter Ney, Rebecca Raeske-Grinch and Elizabeth Salt (Otterbein University, Courtright Memorial Library), Douglas R Smith, Frank Vogel, Mary Wallace, Dave Yount (Mesa Community College).

Special thanks to VK Sethi, author of *Kabir, the weaver of God's Name* and *Mira, the divine lover.* Colleague, mentor, friend, he shared his love for Kabir and years ago filled my mind with images of India's traditions – secular, literary and spiritual – that I've been drawing on ever since. To Louise Hilger, who offered me my first job in the world of publishing and was a model of focus, dedication and hard work. And to hundreds of writers and all my language teachers over the years: a big thank you for kindling and keeping alight my enjoyment of words, literature and meaning.

My appreciation to various translators whose published versions of mystic texts helped me as I finalized my own: Gopal Singh (Adi Granth), Shiv Dhatt (Adi Granth, Bahu, Soami Ji of Agra), KN Upadhyaya (Dadu, Ravidas), VK Sethi (Mira, Kabir), Isaac Ezekiel (Paltu); to the University of Chicago for digital treasure: dsal.uchicago.edu/dictionaries/; and to BibleHub.com for easy access to multiple translations of the Bible and New Testament, including concordances, literal translations and lexicons Hebrew and Greek.

Profound gratitude for my family! My parents, John and Karis Guinness – their love, positive support and open-minded approach to all religions paved the way for everything that has followed; my grandparents, especially Grace and Geraldine, all born in the 1800s – pioneers in their own generation who rose above limitations and convention in pursuit of their dreams; and my two sisters, Lindis and Chloe – special appreciation for all their love, and for lifelong friendship, encouragement, shared interests, and so many good memories…

The selections in *The Inner Way* give a tiny hint of the extraordinary nature of a true spiritual teacher. Gratitude to my master and his successor cannot be expressed in words… The masters say “Love needs to be packaged as meditation,” so may the grace of daily effort remain to our very last breath!

ABOUT THE EDITOR/TRANSLATOR

In 1975 Anthea Guinness went to India on a 9-month Hindi scholarship and stayed for twenty-nine years. She studied, taught, translated – and copy-edited books on the bhakti tradition. With a PhD in comparative religion, she is the founder of Salt River Publishing and lives now in Arizona.

Loërd, thou clepedest me
And I not ne answerëd thee
But wordës slow and sleepy:
"Thole yiet! Thole a little!"
But 'yiet' and 'yiet' was endëless,
And 'thole a little' a long way is.

Lord, you called me
And I answered you only
With words slow and sleepy:
"Be patient! Just a little while more!"
But 'yet a little while' was endless,
And 'be patient' goes on forever.[183]

APPRECIATION

Thank you

for buying a copy of this book.

Available at Amazon.com

and

SaltRiverPublishing.com

Discount available at the SRP estore

SALT RIVER BOOKLIST

Global Library Books

- Janice Fletcher, EdD – *Teach with Spirit: A teacher's inward journey guide*
- Anthea Guinness – *The inner way: A mystic anthology of songpoems, stories, reflections* SUITABLE FOR AGE 13 ON UP
- Anthea Guinness – *Wake up! if you can: Sayings of Kabir with reflections and mystic stories*
- Anthea Guinness – *Soami Ji of Agra answering questions: Mystic teachings on the path of inner sound,* 2 volumes

Tuppany Books

- Shanan Harrell – *Stumbling towards enlightenment: A Yoga 101 collection* *K
- Rosemary Rawson – *Coming of age: Notes from the front line of aging* *K
- Elley-Ray Tsipolitis – *Butterfly kisses: Quotes for daily motivation and renewal*

Pocketbooks

- *Dawn has come: Songpoems of Paltu*

*K for KINDLE

Eye of an Artist Books

- Greg Meyer – ***Arizona Places: Otherworldly and beautiful***

Beyond Borders Books

- Dyan Dubois – ***Rajasthan Suite Memory*** *(a novel)* *K

New Moon Books ***for children***

- Tia Pleiman, Village Voices series – ***I am the rainbow, With my hands, Color in the book, In my dreams***

Independent Publications

Salt River assistance with editing, book design, composition, cover design

- Rosemary Rawson – ***Dark bread and dancing***
- Chloe Faith Wordsworth – ***Quantum change, Spiral up!*** and eleven other Resonance Repatterning books

www.SaltRiverPublishing.com

COLOPHON

Typefaces: Adobe Brioso Pro (designed by Robert Slimbach), Vatican (designed by Alan Meeks), Adobe Jensen Pro (designed by Nicolas Jensen and Robert Slimbach), Trajan Pro (designed by Carol Twombly)
Software: Adobe InDesign
Book Design: Carol White of Salt River Publishing – *email:* carol@saltriverpublishing.com
Composition: Anthea Guinness and Carol White
Cover Photo, used with permission: The Long Man, Windover Hill, Wilmington, East Sussex, UK, taken by website builder Rune Clausen of www.runemester.dk
Cover Design: Carol White and Anthea Guinness
Printer: createspace.com
Printing method: Print-on-Demand (POD) digital printing
Paper: Library quality
Binding: Perfect binding

www.SaltRiverPublishing.com

SALT RIVER

Salt River Publishing believes in encouraging artists and publishing professionals to come together and reach their empowered "Yes!"

Salt River was established as a no-profit publisher with the idea of helping writers, translators, poets, graphic artists and photographers bring their work into publishable form and make 100% of the profit on their book sales.

And to promote, for free, the expertise of publishing professionals whose services an author might need when they have a book in the making.

We publish books that inspire, encourage and entertain, including children's books – and books that deepen the understanding of mysticism.

Do you have one?

READER RESPONSE TO SALT RIVER BOOKS

"So many problems are spiritual in nature. And healing often involves finding meaning, purpose and spiritual uplift. The right words at the right time can turn a life around. Therapists and practitioners can point the way for clients who are seeking meaning; writers and artists have the opportunity to share in that work. Thank you, Salt River."

Printed in Great Britain
by Amazon